I0605518

A Guide to
Regency Dress

'Hilary Davidson's ability to combine precise scholarly rigour with lively, engaging prose would make Jane Austen herself proud. I am a huge fan of her work and this is an excellent culmination of her trilogy on Regency dress. Bringing together material knowledge and archival research, no historian should be without it!'

Amber Butchart, Curator and historian

'Connecting surviving historical garments, their contemporary depictions and the names given to them at that time completes the triangle of evidence needed to understand the dress of any period. Hilary Davidson brilliantly achieves this for Regency dress within these pages.'

Jenny Tiramani, Principal, The Historical School of Dress

DR HILARY DAVIDSON is associate professor, and Chair of MA Fashion and Textile Studies at the Fashion Institute of Technology, New York. She has curated, lectured, broadcast, and published extensively in her field. She is author of *Dress in the Age of Jane Austen: Regency Fashion* and *Jane Austen's Wardrobe*.

A Guide to

Regency Dress

from Corsets and Breeches to Bonnets and Muslins

HILARY DAVIDSON

YALE UNIVERSITY PRESS
New Haven and London

First published by Yale University Press 2025
302 Temple Street, P.O. Box 209040, New Haven CT 06520-9040
47 Bedford Square, London WC1B 3DP

For information about this and other Yale University Press publications, please contact:
U.S. Office: sales.press@yale.edu yalebooks.com
Europe Office: sales@yaleup.co.uk yalebooks.co.uk

Project Editor: Daphne Fordham-Smith
Senior Production Controller: Leonie Kellman
Text designed and set in Scotch Modern and Figgins Sans by Tetragon, London

Printed and bound in the Czech Republic by FINIDR

Library of Congress Control Number: 2025939441

A catalogue record for this book is available from the British Library.

Authorised Representative in the EU: Easy Access System Europe, Mustamäe tee 50, 10621 Tallinn, Estonia, gpsr.requests@easproject.com

ISBN 978-0-300-28241-2

10 9 8 7 6 5 4 3 2 1

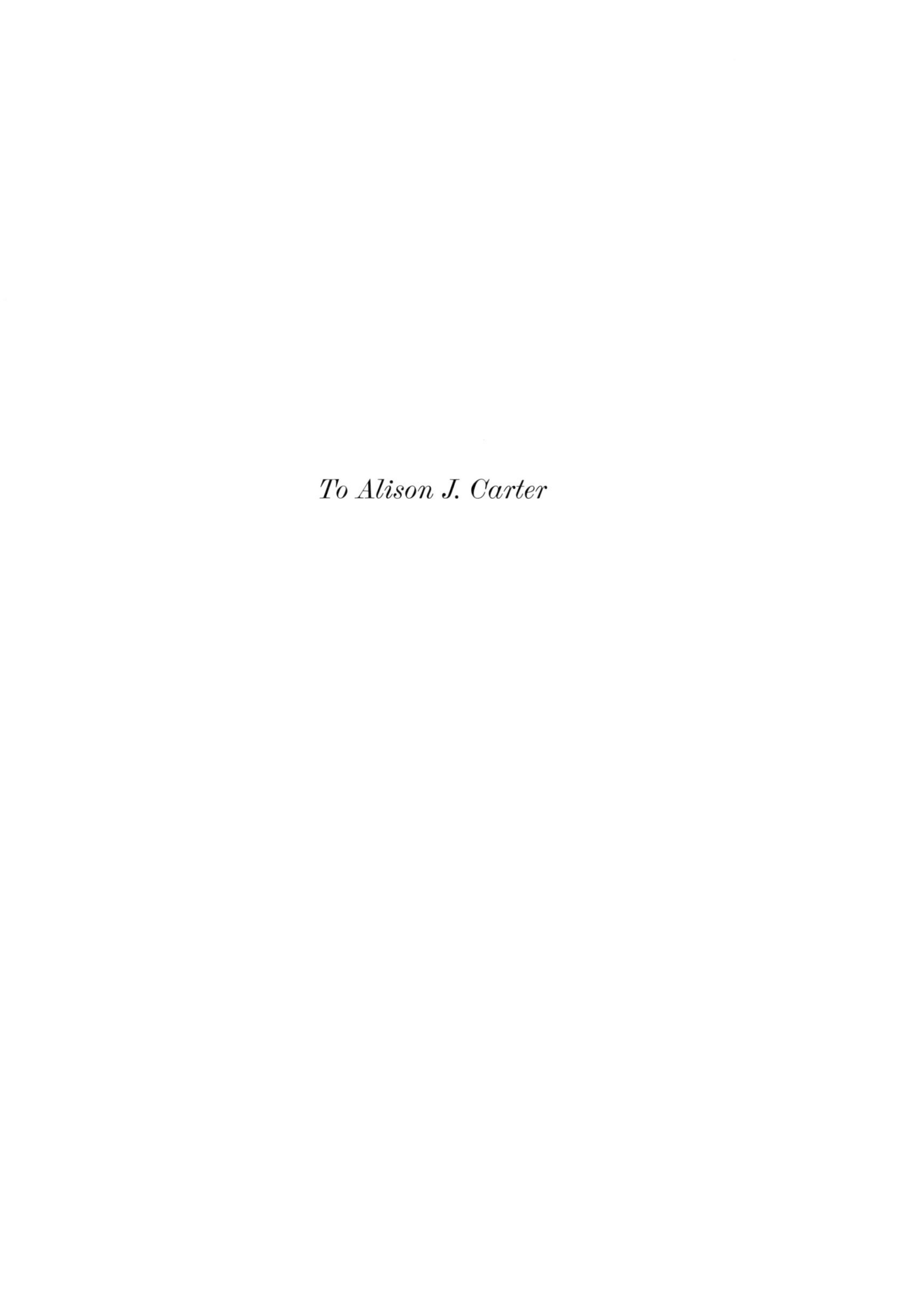

To Alison J. Carter

CONTENTS

INTRODUCTION

'. . . the thin slippers and muslin robes of old time were foolish, fragile, and poetical.'[1]

ELIZABETH GASKELL,
'A Fear for the Future', *Fraser's Magazine*, 1859

Welcome to the rich and fascinating world of Regency dress and textiles. This period of British history, starting in the late, revolutionary years of the eighteenth century and flowing into the turbulent and changeable early nineteenth century, is among the most distinctive for what people wore, how they wore it, and what their garments and accessories were made of. The era has inspired people ever since, from William Makepeace Thackeray who wrote his novel *Vanity Fair* reflecting back from the 1840s on the Napoleonic Wars between Britain and France (1803–15), to Charlotte Brontë, whom historian Kate Faber Oestreich has recently suggested set Jane Eyre in 1812 – the same year as Jane Austen's incalculably important *Pride and Prejudice* – not in the 1830s or 40s as usually supposed. The muslin gowns, high waistline, tight breeches and well-cut coats have inspired every subsequent generation. 'Directoire' styles appeared in the late 1880s, inspired by fashions in the late 1790s immediately after the French Revolution, during

France's Directory period, while the names for both 'Directoire' and 'Empire' fashions (with waistlines just under the bust) only emerged from Parisian designers around 1907, the latter taking its name from Napoleon's First Empire established in 1804. These terms were never used at the time. In English, the appreciation of Jane Austen's six completed novels published between 1811 and 1817, which grew throughout the nineteenth and early twentieth centuries, motivated Georgette Heyer's wildly popular Regency romances written between 1935 and 1972. This lineage of historically inspired romantic fiction led directly to the exponentially greater popularity of the Netflix streaming series *Bridgerton* (2020–ongoing), based on Julia Quinn's novels (2000–6). On the more historical side, the legion of Austen adaptations for screen, starting in 1938, have created their own lively and highly influential visions of the dressed Regency world – a legacy that shows no sign of abating.

It is reasonable to assume that most people first encounter Regency fashion now through some kind of filmed costume drama. This in turn relates to groups such as the various Jane Austen Societies around the world, with many members who make and wear Regency costumes; and the year-on-year growth of re-enactment societies for the Napoleonic Wars and associated eras (especially the War of 1812 in the United States). Add to this the explosion of online videos and the 'Costube' communities using platforms such as YouTube to share information on making historic costumes, and there has never been such an interest in dress of the years between around 1795 to 1820.

Those who have already read my first two books, *Dress in the Age of Jane Austen: Regency Fashion* and *Jane Austen's Wardrobe*, may wonder what more I can possibly say about Regency dress. I wondered this myself and am pleased to say the answer is 'quite a lot'. The first two books focused on the life and times of Jane Austen and were the result of fifteen years' worth of Regency dress research. The purpose of this book is to share that broader, non-Austen-related research in an accessible and practical way as a guide to Regency dress, for both men and women, including areas of adornment such as hair, beauty and jewellery, and the textiles and trimmings essential to creating clothing. The text is concerned with dress of the professional, middle-class and aristocratic peoples of the United Kingdom, roughly gentlemen and gentlewomen, although most of the sources are English (more information on Scottish, Welsh and Irish dress, specifically, can be found in *Dress in the Age of Jane Austen*). Even after my years of experience in this subject, I learnt a lot of new information about Regency fashions while researching this guide, and am pleased to be able to share it.

BACKGROUND INFORMATION

The time period this book covers is what I call the 'long Regency'. In academic work, 'Regency' is a flexible concept, a summary of the early nineteenth century in Britain and its colonies, with some authors starting the period at the French Revolution in 1789, and others finishing it at Queen Victoria's accession to the throne in 1837. It is not the technical definition of the Regency, which lasted between 1811 and 1820 as George, Prince of Wales, became Prince Regent and ruled in place of his father George III, incapacitated by illness. When the king died in 1820, the prince became George IV (the *Bridgerton* screen series is, strictly speaking, not set in the Regency period, as in its alternative history timeline Queen Charlotte rules in place of her stricken husband and the Act of Regency has not taken place). However, 'Regency' is the easiest and most understandable way of summarising this period. 'Late Georgian' would reach all the way to 1830 and sounds rather dry; 'Napoleonic Wars period' doesn't deal with the interesting style changes occurring after the emperor's final defeat at the Battle of Waterloo in 1815; and French or American descriptions such as 'post-Revolutionary' or 'Federalist' are irrelevant to the British context.

Much of the development in clothing during this period reflected larger national and global events. This 'long Regency' in Britain was shaped by significant political, cultural and technological changes during the late eighteenth and early nineteenth centuries. Following the shock to Britain of losing its American colonies in the War of Independence (1775–83), the late eighteenth-century political landscape was dominated by the aftermath of the French Revolution (1789–93), which led to a rise in radical political movements in Britain, advocating for reform and greater democratic rights. The ongoing wars with France beginning in 1793 galvanised national unity but also intensified a struggle between conservative and liberal ideals within Britain. The Act for the Union of Great Britain and Ireland created the United Kingdom in 1801. Two years later, the Napoleonic Wars began, including a series of conflicts between Britain and Napoleon Bonaparte's aggressively expanding French Empire, and involving various coalitions of European nations. They concluded with Napoleon's defeat by forces led by the Duke of Wellington at the Battle of Waterloo in June 1815, and the deposed emperor's subsequent exile. This brought both relief and economic hardship to Britain.

Culturally, this period was an exciting time for literature, art and philosophy. The Romantic movement emerged in art and philosophy as a response to the ongoing Industrial Revolution and Enlightenment rationalism. Poets such as William Wordsworth, Samuel Taylor Coleridge and Lord Byron emphasised emotion, nature and individualism. Their works often reflected the turbulent political climate and a longing for social change. Significant contributions from female novelists also helped shape the literary landscape, most notably Jane Austen, who has become the defining Regency author, with her novels offering incisive commentary on marriage, class and women's lives. Mary Shelley gained prominence with *Frankenstein* (1818), and Ann Radcliffe's Gothic novels such as *The Mysteries of Udolpho* (1794) set the stage for future Gothic fiction. Frances Burney continued to affect Regency intellectual culture with her explorations in novels of female agency, though her most notable works were published earlier, such as *Evelina* (1778), while Anglo-Irish Maria Edgeworth was one of the most widely read authors in the early nineteenth-century United Kingdom. In addition to literature, visual arts flourished, with artists such as J.M.W. Turner and John Constable capturing the changing landscape of Britain and the effects of increasing industrialisation.

Technological advancements during this period were transformative, marking the early stages of the Industrial Revolution. Textile manufacturing saw significant advancements, with inventions of the spinning jenny and the power loom dramatically increasing fabric production capabilities. This period experienced a general rise in mechanisation, which changed labour dynamics and contributed to the growth of factory systems, leading to both economic prosperity and social challenges. At the same time, British naval power was unrivalled, essential in securing victories during the Napoleonic Wars. The Royal Navy's dominance ensured control over trade routes and colonial interests, with significant battles including Trafalgar (1805) affirming its supremacy. This period established Britain as the pre-eminent maritime and mercantile force of the nineteenth century, which greatly helped the development of its empire as the century progressed.

FASHION

Following developments in wider culture, fashionable style in the long Regency saw a transformation from Classicism, based on order, harmony, balance, rational structure and perfection, towards the feeling, individualistic, intuitive, picturesque Romanticism. There was a freshness and modernity in Regency dress. It made a break with stiff, artificial silhouettes, then concerned itself with an idealised relationship to the natural body. Applying art historical terms to fashion, the linear, austere Classical aesthetics of *c*.1800 exploited the body's shape by draping over a 'natural' form. 'Neo-classical' was a phrase applied to Regency decorative and visual arts only retrospectively in the 1880s, as a term of disapproval. The style at the time was simply the 'true' or 'correct' taste, reacting against Rococo frivolity. By 1820, the shift towards a more expressive, curving, consciously feminine Romantic or Gothic style was firmly established for women, now exploiting the gown's shape with stiffer surfaces and increased decoration. Even men's fashions became more voluminous and curvilinear.

The growth of historicism throughout the later eighteenth century found full expression in Regency dress. Fashion fantasies bridged distances in time and space to embody concepts of the Classical ancient world; of the Gothicised Baroque, Renaissance and Middle Ages; of exoticism and the picturesque foreign and 'Oriental' worlds (a fantasy amalgam of Asian, African and Middle Eastern cultures) brought closer by the ongoing wars. Clothing modes simultaneously cast off fashion's immediate past, yet sought further back in history for old dress to be made new again, reflecting in clothing many of Romanticism's core aesthetic concerns. Many passing novel styles recorded in magazines' fashion descriptions relate to these three main stylistic influences of antiquity, history and non-European worlds. British society started looking back on itself and responding to its own history, considering the past from the future.

It is important to remember that not every person adopted or wore fashionable clothing at the same rate. The trend-setting attire of social leaders, or innovations in cut, colour, trimming or textile, took a while to filter through society. It was not necessarily top down but had more to do with access to resources for fashion, and a willingness to engage with them, which every individual decided differently. The middle classes in particular were concerned with being neither too far ahead of nor too far behind fashion, aiming for a happy medium. Age and convention seem to have had as much to do with fashionable adoption as money and class. Scholars such as John Styles have shown that young labouring people were often as interested in consuming fashion as young gentlepeople were, and both did so to the extent that their local resources and incomes allowed. So much new fashionable change came through watching what other people were wearing. While a gentleman or gentlewoman had the advantage of travel, and metropolitan correspondents, their working compatriots could still observe other people's dress keenly in their local town and at county fairs. In visual sources, older people of all social levels are frequently shown in clothing of more eighteenth-century style, twenty years or more behind fashions of other figures in the image. People develop a certain kind of comfort with the clothing they are most used to, and some seem to have retained their previous dress conventions well into the nineteenth century, for reasons of preference, economy, or disinterest in change. Other older people kept up with fashion, however, which sometimes then attracted criticism as being inappropriate for their years. A happy medium is sometimes neither happy nor medium.

Clothing was a much more significant investment as a proportion of disposable income than it is now, with the textiles themselves being most of the garment's value. I encourage readers to have a look at the Textiles and Trimmings section to familiarise themselves with this material aspect of dress, which was as important to Regency consumers as the style and suitability of fashions. The difference between whether a silk fabric was sarcenet, taffeta or satin really mattered to those who wore them. People knew the exact qualities of textiles, and how they would last or wear, which they brought to bear in their purchases. Clothes were expected to be worn for a number of years, with alterations and repairs as needed to keep them functioning and fashionable.

Bear in mind also that not everyone called the same garment the same thing at the same time. If you find yourself reading through entries and encountering confusion about, for instance, when a spencer is a spencer and when it is a short jacket, this reflects the multitudes of names and meanings in use at the time. Britain has significant regional language variations within the isles to begin with, and Anglophones from various countries today interpret clothing words such as 'thong', 'vest' and 'suspender' quite differently. I have done my best to sort out the subtle differences, but some items had multiple descriptions. The undergarment that filled in the chest of a woman's gown, for example, could be called variously a shirt, habit-shirt, collared neck-handkerchief, shirt handkerchief, tucker or chemisette. Other words have multiple meanings. Petticoat was a general word for any kind of skirt not attached as part of a gown, which could extend from plain garments used as underwear to splendid, richly embellished skirts for court ensembles. Just to add more confusion, 'petticoat' was sometimes abbreviated to 'coat' in accounts. Other changes of language – for instance, the slow shift from 'gown' to 'dress', or the rise in French fashion descriptions after the Battle of Waterloo in 1815 – can be traced as part of larger cultural changes. I have indicated these where possible. The long Regency is a fascinating period precisely because it contained so much change and experimentation, both in the wider world and the field of fashion, even if trying to map the developments can be complex.

The images illustrating each entry are taken from a range of historical sources, all of which have their own quirks and show different ways of wearing clothes – the ideal, the actual, and, in some cases, the ludicrous. These include fashion plates from periodicals, engravings from pocketbooks, details of satirical pictures and caricatures that exaggerate for effect, and paintings in oil, gouache and watercolour that aim for lifelike or flattering versions of their sitters. These are complemented by historic objects, which are wonderful resources for texture and construction but usually do not demonstrate, in themselves, how the items looked or behaved when worn, or how they were accessorised to create an ensemble. Together, however, these sources build up a full picture of Regency dress.

I have consciously tried to include images of people of colour, who were present in Britain during this period in great numbers, and who came from many cultural and geographic origins. The British navy itself was profoundly multicultural. However, visual records of white people dominate for the middling and upper classes. In addition, many illustrations show people of colour, particularly Black people, employed as servants, or depicted in grotesquely racist ways which exclude their use. As I was looking specifically for examples of British fashionable dress, the many lovely portraits from the French-colonised West Indies or Dutch colonies in the East Indies could not be included. There may also be portraits now available that will later turn out to show people who in real life were of colour, but who 'passed' as white, or whose whiteness was exaggerated for the portrait. I very much hope that future research will uncover more of the stories and pictures of the full spectrum of British society in this period, and thus further help combat the negative biases many people of colour still experience when participating in history or costuming communities.

HOW TO USE THIS BOOK

This book is part guide, part glossary, and part dictionary. It is aimed at people with no prior knowledge of Regency dress as much as those who work with fashion history, including costumers, designers and curators. You may have picked up this book because you are going to a fancy-dress event and do not know where to start, or perhaps you are tracking down a specific obscure textile reference. The contents are intended to help everyone. The book is arranged in sections giving alphabetised definitions of clothing and accessories for Women, then Men, followed by mixed-gender information on Hair and Beauty, then Jewellery, and it finishes by cataloguing the Textiles and Trimmings that were the material components of fashion.

KEY POINTS

- Each section starts with its own general introduction.
- The entries are illustrated by selected images to help explain the text. Not every entry has a picture and I have concentrated on lesser-known objects.
- General indications are given in places about how common, usual or prevalent a detail of dress or textile was. There will always be exceptions in historic examples, and the generalisations are intended to be more of a guide.
- Within the text, an asterisk before a word – for example, *bonnet – invites the reader to look up the relevant entry in the glossary.
- Where an item is used by both women and men but the term has a different meaning, an (F) for female or (M) for male is added after the word to avoid confusion between the separate entries. (HB) does the same thing for hair and beauty, as do (J) for jewellery and (T) for textiles. A gender binary was strict in the period, but readers can interpret the clothing as they prefer.
- Dates are avoided within the entries unless they are relevant to the introduction of a style or textile.
- Variations in spellings and word combinations found in period sources are given after the main headword, which is the most common variant either in the period or now.

All the information presented here has been gained by many years of research. I've looked at hundreds of original garments, consulted fellow experts, and scoured through thousands of texts, books, novels and scholarly works, including reading all the fashion commentary in the contemporary magazines *La Belle Assemblée* and *The Repository of Arts, Literature, Commerce, Manufactures, Fashions, and Politics*, up to 1820. There are very few footnotes in the text – *Dress in the Age of Jane Austen* is a feast of footnotes, for those who like them – but every entry is as accurate as I can make it with the resources available. Sometimes the definitions surprised me, once a new context in a trade journal came up, or an offhand note on fashion. Any mistakes are absolutely my own, and I welcome any new or corrective resources.

Once again, there is far more information and subject matter out there than I can possibly squeeze into a useful book. The dress of servants, labouring people, children, the military and navy, and professionals such as doctors, lawyers and the clergy, is not included, nor is ceremonial clothing. I have included context details where necessary, such as the customs around mourning dress, but mostly the entries focus on defining what a garment, piece of jewellery or textile item was, what it looked like, and what it was made of. For a broader overview of the social and cultural background, please see *Dress in the Age of Jane Austen*, which includes subjects such as shopping, and how clothes were made and cleaned.

FURTHER RESOURCES

CURRENCY

The prices of British goods were expressed in pounds, shillings and pence (indicated by the abbreviations L, s. and d.). In that currency, there were 20s. to £1, and 12d. to 1s.; £1 was therefore worth 240d. A guinea was £1 1s., or 252d. As an approximate indication of values during the Regency period, the average annual income for an English labourer in 1800 was around £15–20. £20 was a year's salary for a butler, exclusive of food, board and some clothing. In 1800, 21 per cent of families in England and Wales had an annual income over £100; 7 per cent had an income over £200; and those enjoying an income of £1,000 or more per annum comprised only 1.25 per cent of the population – about 28,000 families. Income over £150 per annum put a family roughly in the top 10 per cent of earners.

MEASUREMENTS

Dimensions have been given in the imperial measures in use in Britain at the time: the standard inch and yard, and their contemporary divisions such as fractions of a yard, or nails, followed, where appropriate, by a metric equivalent in parentheses. For more general purposes: 1 inch = 2.54 cm and 1 yard (3 feet) = 91.44 cm. The metric system was created in France in 1799. Sometimes textiles can reveal their origin after this date by a precise centimetre measurement.

PERIODICALS AND MAGAZINES

If you would like to know more about British fashions in this period, the following contemporaneous periodicals and magazines are increasingly available online. Reading the descriptive text that originally accompanied each image is essential to understanding the fashions as people of the time would have, especially regarding the fabrics:

La Belle Assemblée; or, Bell's Court and Fashionable Magazine (published 1806–37)
The Gallery of Fashion (published 1794–1803)
Ladies Fashionable Repository (published 1809–29)
The Lady's Magazine (published 1770–1847)
The Lady's Monthly Museum; or, Polite Repository of Amusement and Instruction (published 1798–1832)
The Magazine of Female Fashions of London & Paris (published 1798–1806), continued until 1809 as *Record of Fashion and Court Elegance*
The Repository of Arts, Literature, Commerce, Manufactures, Fashions, and Politics (published 1809–29, often referred to as 'Ackermann's Repository' after its publisher, Rudolph Ackermann)

I also recommend novelist Candice Hern's website, where she has created an excellent digitised library of fashion plates from contemporary periodicals, and transcribed the text: https://candicehern.com/regency-world/collections/fashion-prints. This is a great place to discover some of the more eccentric and extreme inventions of Regency fashion without reading through a whole magazine.

FURTHER ONLINE RESOURCES

All Things Georgian https://georgianera.wordpress.com
Jane Austen's World https://janeaustensworld.com
The Lady's Magazine (1770–1819): Patterns of Perfection https://ladysmagazine.omeka.net
The Race and Regency Lab https://www.raceandregency.org

SELECTED PUBLICATIONS

Any historical research builds on the careful work of others. I have found the publications of Edward Maeder, Deb Salisbury, Penelope Byrde, Alison J. Carter, Florence M. Montgomery, and especially C. Willett and Phillis Cunnington most helpful for this book, plus many other thoughtful writers from and about the years covered. Please also refer to the Bibliography section on p. 235.

The following books are particularly recommended for those who wish to explore the world of Regency dress and textiles further:

Ashmore, Sonia, *Muslin* (London: V&A Publishing, 2012)
Batchelor, Jennie, and Alison Larkin, *Jane Austen Embroidery: Authentic Embroidery Projects for Modern Stitchers* (London: Pavilion, 2020)
Byrde, Penelope, *Jane Austen Fashion: Fashion and Needlework in the Works of Jane Austen* (Ludlow: Moonrise Press, 2008)
Cunnington, C. Willett, and Phillis Cunnington, *Handbook of English Costume in the Nineteenth Century* (London: Faber and Faber, 1970)
Davidson, Hilary, *Dress in the Age of Jane Austen: Regency Fashion* (London and New Haven, CT: Yale University Press, 2019)
Davidson, Hilary, *Jane Austen's Wardrobe* (London and New Haven, CT: Yale University Press, 2023)
Downing, Sarah Jane, *Fashion in the Time of Jane Austen* (Oxford: Shire Publications, 2010)

Johnston, Lucy, *19th-Century Fashion in Detail* (London: V&A Publishing, 2016)

Le Bourhis, Katell (ed.), *The Age of Napoleon: Costume from Revolution to Empire, 1789–1815* (New York: Metropolitan Museum of Art, 1989)

Montgomery, Florence M., *Textiles in America, 1650–1870: A Dictionary Based on Original Documents, Prints and Paintings, Commercial Records, American Merchants' Papers, Shopkeepers' Advertisements, and Pattern Books with Original Swatches of Cloth* (New York: W.W. Norton & Co., 2007)

O'Brien, Alden (ed.), *'An Agreeable Tyrant': Fashion after the Revolution* (Washington, DC: DAR Museum, 2016)

Percoco, Cassidy, *Regency Women's Dress: Techniques and Patterns 1800–1830* (London: B.T. Batsford, 2015)

Ribeiro, Aileen, *The Art of Dress: Fashion in England and France 1750 to 1820* (New Haven, CT: Yale University Press, 1995)

Salisbury, Deb (ed.), *Fabric à la Romantic Regency: A Glossary of Fabrics from Original Sources 1795–1836* (Abbott, TX: The Mantua-Maker Historical Sewing Patterns, 2013)

WOMEN

'The *Cabinet of Fashion* . . . will form a half-yearly Record of the *Female Dresses* of the Country, that will be hereafter an object, at least, of amusing, and perhaps, of useful Reference.'[2]

The Lady's Monthly Museum, 1798

A lovely poem from 1810 called 'How to Pack a Lady's Portmanteau' gives an idea of what the essential clothing and accessories for women were, and also in roughly what order they were worn:

With linen and stockings, and shoes first begin,
Then your Night-cloaths and Petticoats neatly put in.
Next your Dresses compleat, for each part of the day,
With your Handkerchiefs, Caps, all in Gala array,
Then your Ribbands, Fans, Flowers and Gloves long and short,
With your Coombs, and your brushes of every sort,
And snug in your corner your Trinket-box place,
No Cosmeticks you want with that beautiful face,
Some Needles, and Thread, with your Thimble combine,
For one stitch timely set in the end may save nine,
A spare pair of Garters and Lace add to these,
For the rest I will leave you to do as you please.[3]

The 'linen' in the first line is her *chemise, *smock or *shift – all names for the same basic tunic-like undergarment worn against the body. 'Linen' in this sense is a collective word that could encompass

John Constable,
Mrs James Pulham Sr (Frances Amys), *1818*

other intimate underwear made of the fabric, including the lady's *stays or *corset for bust support and figure shaping. Perhaps the male author is decorously not mentioning these by name, or else the lady will be wearing the ones already on her body the whole time. *Petticoats went underneath the dress or *gown, and on top it was accessorised with *handkerchiefs, *caps, and other *bonnets and *headwear. 'Ribbands' (*ribbons), fans, *artificial flowers, and long or short *gloves all contributed to styling an ensemble. *Combs and brushes are dealt with in the Hair and Beauty chapter. What 'trinkets' might comprise is to be discovered in Jewellery. A 'spare pair' of *garters to hold up *stockings tells us that the lady is already wearing one set. The *lace could be many things, from a *staylace to a *tucker or other lace-edged or embroidered accessory. The male version of this poem is presented in the next chapter (see p. 93). Comparing the two parts shows women evidently had more essential clothes and accessories than men.

But what form did all these bits and pieces take? On the one hand, the basic styles of Regency female fashions are easy to describe. From around 1795, more or less, adult women wore gowns, with the waistline under the bust, fairly straight skirts, a range of neckline styles, long or short sleeves, shoes with low or no heels, their hair always up, a cap indoors and a bonnet or hat when they went outdoors, and many kinds of jackets and coats as outerwear, including *spencers, *pelisses and *shawls. In patriotic words from the early century: 'The formal habits, and cumbrous ornaments of [British women's] ancestors, have long and happily given place to the Grecian drapery and gently-flowing robes of softest texture. Nature and simplicity are now in unison with taste and fashion. . . .'[4] On the other hand, the sheer quantity of variations upon these structural themes is incalculable. Due to the rapid changes in manufacturing, construction, politics, textiles and style, it is one of the most quickly evolving aesthetic and technical periods in the history of fashion. The reality of this period's dress for those who lived through these years further competes with the versions depicted in popular culture, especially screen adaptations and dramas, which create a robust but often ahistorical vision of Regency fashion in people's imaginations.

This section is an attempt to define the major garments, accessories and embellishments that British women wore. I say attempt, because they were an inventive lot at this time, and tracing the twists, turns and novelties of dress is no easy task, further complicated by multiplicities of names for similar garments. Even those familiar with this fashion period, therefore, will likely find information new to them, as I did while researching. I have not been able to include every passing fashionable whim, especially in the way of headwear. The numbers of melon bonnets, Tekeli caps, Alexina helmets, Zealand coats, Grecian frocks, Flemish bonnets and ever so many more, promulgated especially in fashion magazines, are passing novelties or styles of a moment. 'All nations are ransacked to equip a modern fine lady', as *The Mirror of the Graces* put it.[5] Where a variation appears regularly across the years, such as a *gipsy hat, it is included. Sorting out what something is becomes even more confusing when names and fabrics, or fabric types, are combined, as with the jockey beaver hats of 1806, or a transparent striped Merino crape in 1812. Colour names and definitions are excluded for the same reason. There were so many colour combinations, names, shades and fads that it is difficult to quantify and attach firm meanings.

There are further complexities in attempting to untangle the differences between the ideal etiquettes of dress for different times of day and life events, and how people actually interpreted them. Regency fashion journalism is replete with descriptions of *visiting dress, *walking dress, *morning dress, *promenade dress, *curricle dress, *carriage dress, *dinner dress, *opera dress, ball dress, *evening dress and *court dress – and every combination of these styles, such as visiting walking dress. A lady would have to possess equal quantities of wealth and vigour to keep up with these ostensible requirements. Fashion reportage, then as now, exaggerated the importance of minute differences in style in order to promote novelty and sales. The feminine-slanted magazine quoted above was correct in its conjectures of forming a useful reference, though I doubt the editors considered its becoming so from a distance of over two hundred years in the future.

The reality for wearers appears to have been simpler, with clothing considered as *undress, *half-dress, or *dress. The biggest distinction in Regency sartorial convention was between 'undress' day clothing and evening or 'full' dress, often just called 'dress'. *The Mirror of the Graces* outlined the regulations of custom according to time of day: 'In the morning the arms and bosom must be completely covered to the throat and wrists. From the dinner-hour to the termination of the day, the arms, to a graceful height above the elbow, may be bare; and the neck and shoulders unveiled as far as delicacy will allow.'[6] *The Repository of Arts* made fun of the same hierarchy by pointing out the contradiction inherent in the names; that 'the *undress* of the present day consists of a comfortable kind of habiliment closed round the neck and covering the arms; that the *half-dress* is rather more open and exposed; and that the *full-dress* scarcely admits of any covering at all, but in common language would be called complete nakedness'.[7] Undress was for home, and private or informal activities. 'The intermediate order of dress', or half-dress – which was rarely called such by people in personal communications – was suitable for daywear outside the house, or public activities before dinner or evening.[8] I have done my best to explain the nuances between each order of dress. If in doubt, it is easiest to consider that middle-class women were most often concerned with merely dress or undress, defined partly as clothing worn during the day by contrast to the more formal evening dress they changed into even for family dinners.

Throughout, I call the main item of female clothing – comprising bodice, sleeves and skirt – a 'gown' rather than a 'dress', both for clarity of reference and in line with historical use. As 'dress' is a noun and a verb, and both singular and plural, it can be hard to pinpoint the earliest instances of 'a dress', meaning the women's main body garment, instead of the whole ensemble. 'Dress', for much of this time and as in the opening quote (see p. 27), meant the whole ensemble, such as walking dress or carriage dress. The first unambiguous usage I have found for 'dress' as a garment dates to 1802, in the caption to a fashion plate. The reference needs to be read in context to work out if the word means an ensemble or an item. This matches the change over the same time from the professional women who made female clothing being called 'mantuamakers', after the popular eighteenth-century gown style, to being called 'dressmakers', considered more modern and genteel by the mid-1810s. 'Modiste' was a French term not used in English at this time. By the 1820s, 'a gown' is more usually 'a dress' at about the same rates as mantua- to dressmaker usage. Some middle-class women made their own body garments such as gowns, but they more often employed a professional. Female woollen tailored garments such as *riding-habits were made by male tailors, while women generally sewed their own linen undergarments and accessories, employed a seamstress (who sewed linens only, distinct from dressmakers who worked with silks, wools, muslins and other fashion fabrics to make gowns), or bought smaller accessories ready-made from milliners and a wide range of retailers.

One of the most enduring Regency fashion myths is that women dampened muslin gowns to make them cling to their bodies. The wholly untrue idea comes from misconstruing contemporary descriptions commenting that women looked *as if* they had dampened their gowns, not that they *had*. Muslin's soft, slightly fuzzy surface clings to itself and undergarments through static electricity and does not need water to outline the body (quite apart from the impracticalities of keeping a gown evenly damp over the course of an evening).

Another prominent misconception is that women stopped wearing corsets. This one arises from misunderstandings of the differences between stays and corsets for people at the time. Some fashion commentaries talk about women 'leaving off stays', but what they usually mean is that they swapped them for corsets. Stays were heavily boned, geometric, torso-smoothing garments that started falling out of favour in the 1790s when softer, unboned or lightly boned upper-body-support garments with two cups for the breasts became more popular as the new high-waisted styles became dominant, which relied for their success on a high, supported bust. These softer corsets followed and shaped the natural lines of the body and were designed to look *as if* they were not there. Further, the top of the breast gussets could be cut below the nipples, which can be clearly seen through the fabric in many portraits and helped create the illusion of wearing no bust support. Some extremely fashionable women, especially French ones, may have discarded a bust-support garment completely, but it was definitely the exception and not the rule in Britain. A good way to tell if a corset was present underneath a gown in a portrait is if the centre bodice is pinned between the breasts with a brooch, or detected by drags in the fabric (see illustration featuring a brooch in the Jewellery chapter; p. 160). It must have something solid to pin to, and therefore reveals the presence of the corset *busk. There is a wonderful and inventive variety of bust-support options over this 25-year period, including corsets, stays, *jumps, *waistcoats and *Circassian vests. By about 1820, the hourglass shape still associated with corsets was established, and the words 'stays' and 'corset' were nearly interchangeable. Rumours of female tightlacing have also been very much exaggerated. As the waistline was under the bust, there was no point reducing the waist until it became visible again at its natural level in the mid-1820s. In fact, during this period it was male dandies who attracted the most ridicule for trying to achieve a small waist through tight-laced stays, which created a narrow waist contrasting with their broad shoulders.

Researching this book has made it clear that many French-originating words used now to describe fashions of this period were not necessarily in use or common at the time, such as *canezou, *fichu, *chemisette and *cornette. After the final end of the Napoleonic Wars in 1815, French fashion language started to dominate in English. 'The *fichu* and *cornette* (the terms cap and handkerchief are no more to be found in Fashion's vocabulary) . . .', explained one author writing in 1816.[9] These word entries are noted here as coming from French by '(Fr.)' and should be used sparingly for interpretations dating before the later 1810s.

CONSTRUCTION OF GOWNS

In this age of shifting styles, it is important to consider the different construction techniques that accompanied the changing form. There was a striking dependency between style and technique during the long Regency. These developments were not an abstract process of fashionable change, but were responses to the physical dimensions of constructing fashionable dress. Both professional and amateur makers established new methods to do so during this time. All makers of Regency clothing had to address frequent stylistic variations, but they also helped to create them by adopting, inventing and exploring new ways of making their garments. From the late 1790s, makers appear to be exploring techniques and possibilities to achieve the latest style, inventing it as they go. This sense of experimentation about how a front closes, if a back can close, how deep an armhole is cut, whether a seam is straight or curved, if a bodice is lined, if a skirt is pleated or gathered, how the skirt attaches to the bodice, how gathering and tucking create the shape of a bodice, continues through the 1800s and early 1810s in extant garments. By around 1814–15, makers seem to have achieved some consensus about basic construction, and making techniques became more uniform.

Regency dressmaking was finely attuned to the connection between external surfaces and the internal structures of gowns, particularly in the crucial area of the bust and upper torso. This region including breasts, back and armholes required the most accurate fit, as the sleeves and skirt took their proportions from, and attached onto, this foundation. Skirts were initially raised higher on the existing gown bodice when high waists came into fashion, leaving the original longer waist inside in case the line dropped again. But it soon became clear that the change was permanent. The linen bodice lining became unattached from the outer fabric at the front, creating two separate overlapping flaps fitting over the bust. The gown's front skirt attached to the front bodice panel, which was then pinned or buttoned at the shoulders. This apron- or fall-front opening became usual, and the whole style was called the *round gown as it closed in front. From 1795 to around 1800 gowns retained the pleated back bodice, inherited from 1780s fashions, in round gowns and in 'open gowns' with long trains and matching petticoats. By the turn of the nineteenth century, fashion's slimmest lines took the bulk out of the bodice, leaving only the low-set shoulder seam to create a distinctive 'kite'-shaped back. From around 1804 bodices began to be fastened at the centre back with buttons. A gown made with this new type of construction was a 'frock'. The cut dominated from *c.*1810, and by 1820 centuries of front-opening gowns were finally superseded, as most gowns opened at the back. Specific details of the rapid constructional changes over the 25-year period are outlined in the table on pages 36–37.

The high waistline fluctuated in position. From being directly under the bosom at around the turn of the century and through the first decade of the 1800s, it started lowering through the early teens. After 1814–15, waistlines varied widely. Day gowns show them returning almost to the natural waist by the early 1820s. At the same time, many 1815–20 evening gowns have front bodice depths of as little as two and a half inches (6.5 cm), narrower even than the first shortening. The fall-front closing was disappearing by 1810, though daywear kept it for longer. The new integrated bodice allowed for unified decorative treatments at the front, and smoothness was achieved over the bust by using bias cutting and darts. The subtle bodice-shaping methods emerged from refining earlier experimentation with fabric manipulation in the form of pin tucks, gathers, ruching, and the piecing together of trims and fabrics.

In the 1790s sleeves became tighter, fitting to the arm with no gathering at the sleeve head, and increasingly shorter until they reached the height of simplicity as tubes around 1800–5. Thereafter, they gradually became fuller at the sleeve head, starting at the back, and increasing steadily in size to become a true puff by the late 1810s.

A rapid sophistication of cut affected gown skirts. The economical eighteenth-century method of leaving fabric breadths for skirts uncut, joined at their straight, selvedge edges, translated well to the columnar styles of the late 1790s. Gowns from this date have abundant straight skirts pleated at the back. They used up to five widths of fabric in one skirt, creating bulk around the torso, and ending in long trains following the wearer for a good yard or two. Classical formality rapidly narrowed skirts after 1800. Now gowns lost at least one fabric breadth. Gathering attached the skirt to the bodice all the way round, moving further to the back year by year. By the late 1800s dressmakers started cutting gores – long, triangular side pieces – which took bulk from the waistline and added it to the hem. At the same time, trains mainly disappeared, and skirts shortened. 1820 saw women wearing distinctly triangular, bell-shaped gowns, gathered at the back. From the severe, linear, austere simplicity achieved in 1800, a soft, curving femininity was established by the 1820s, one featuring stiffer surfaces with increased decoration. In just over two decades, the cut and conception of women's dress had changed completely.

Women's gown style and

	BODICE	SKIRT	SLEEVES	DETAILS
1795	Lined in linen (body lining). Waistline is rising rapidly. The round gown, closed at the front, is increasing in popularity. Gathered necklines and waists become fashionable, adding bulk. Some pleated backs with no waist seam.	Uncut straight breadths of fabric, usually 2–5. Pleated onto the waistline. Trains are popular, with straight or rounded ends – maximum length *c.*1798–1802. Bulk of fabric distributed around the waist.	Gown sleeves are mostly elbow- length. Either set into the sleevehead smoothly or full gathers. Straight sleeves fit to the arm. If sleeves are long on jackets or bodices the cut is shaped to the arm with a bend at the elbow, cut in two pieces with the seams running from mid-back and mid-front, not the top or under the arm.	Necklines start to be adjustable through draw-strings. This continues until the early 1820s.
1800	The waistline is just below the natural bust. Still lined in a solid fabric. Gathers have replaced pleats. Crossover and straight horizontal necklines popular. Back seams become angled. Shoulder seams dropped to the back. Back neckline lowers. No side seams.	Straight breadths (selvedge to selvedge). Reduction in the number of breadths used: 2–4. Trains still present but shortening, especially in day dress. Gathers at the top of the skirt at the front are disappearing, instead becoming flat where attached to the bodice. Bulk of fabric concentrated at the centre back.	Short, above-elbow or cap sleeves are the most fashionable. Small fullness through gathers at the sleevehead. Muslin dresses have lost the linen sleeve lining.	Some gowns lose their pocket slits. The peak of tubular, straight fashion, though still with some fabric bulk.
1805	Gowns start having back openings. The fall-front or bib fastening is popular. Linen linings pin together over the bosom, then are concealed by a piece of outer gown fabric pinned or buttoned onto the shoulder straps. Waistline under bust. Back seams start to curve, creating characteristic 'kite' shape.	2–3 breadths of straight fabric in the skirt, not always using the selvedge: some pieces are cut from a length. Flat at the centre front of skirt. Bulk of fabric at the back. Gathers have replaced pleats. Trains much shorter.	Sleeves increase slightly in fullness at the sleevehead. Short cap or puffed sleeves are the most fashionable. Sometimes caps are put over longer undersleeves for daywear. Sleeves are deeply set into the bodice.	Gowns of muslin and other transparent fabrics are often unlined, including the bodice. Separate, sometimes coloured slips provide a lining.

construction changes 1795–1820

BODICE	SKIRT	SLEEVES	DETAILS	
Muslin bodices are now unlined. Some other gowns lose their body-lining too. Bodices cut on the straight grain. Bust shaping is controlled through gathers or cut. The waist begins to drop slightly. Back-opening gowns fasten with tapes tied together, or buttons. Back seams curved.	Triangular side gores start to increase, so skirts widen slightly at the hem. Selvedge to selvedge breadths still used. Trains only in court dress.	Sleeves increase in size with the fullness at the sleevehead towards the back. Depth of armhole at the back decreases. Long sleeves in the evening are acceptable, usually cut on the bias.	Muslin and transparent gowns now completely unlined. Applied surface decoration increases, especially bands of fabric. Vandyked decoration is popular.	**1810**
The waist continues to drop for daywear, but rises to its narrowest ever depth for evening wear *c.*1816–18. Bias-cut bodices begin, using darts to shape the fullness. Curved back seams.	Skirts are increasingly triangular. Flounces and hem decorations become popular. Gown skirts shorten to show the petticoat hem.	Sleeves continue to increase in size with gathered or pleated fullness at the sleevehead at the top and back. Depth of armhole at the back decreases.	Sudden increase in the use of haberdashery to trim gowns, especially piping, cording, ribbon, fabric foliage, braids. Rise in number of gauze and net gowns worn over slips.	**1815**
Gowns are now usually back-opening, fastening with buttons or hooks and eyes, or hooks and worked eyelets. Cotton linings cut on the bias.	Skirts are bell-shaped, and always cut with triangular pieces. Stiffening at the hems helps them to stand out, using wadding and interlining. Lots of emphasis on hem decoration. Flat at the front, bulk gathered or pleated into side and back.	Puffed sleeves are normal. Fullness distributed all around the sleevehead. Often cut on the bias.	Cotton starts to appear in tapes and linings. Piping or cording of bodice and sleeve seams becomes popular. Rouleaux decoration made from the same fabric as the gown also popular. Surface decoration increases.	**1820**

Parts of Women's Dress, November 1807

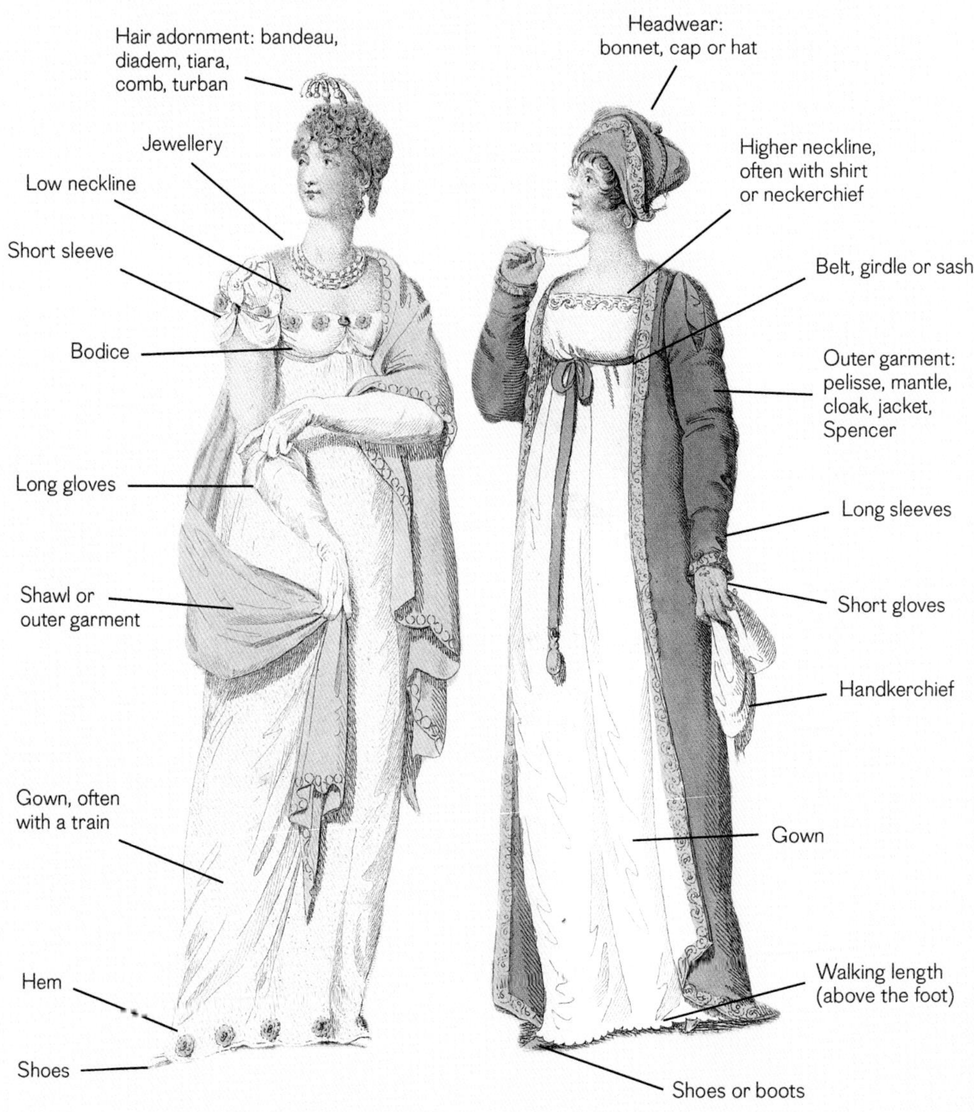

EVENING DRESS **MORNING DRESS**

GLOSSARY

afternoon dress One of the categories of *half-dress, public daywear in the afternoon and early evening, although used as a fashion description far more in magazines than in people's everyday language.

apron (F) (1) A square, rectangular or shaped garment worn at the front of the body, tying around the waist, to protect the clothes underneath, usually made of sturdy or washable textiles, but could also be a non-functional adornment made in fine or embroidered material. (2) The rectangular front of a gown that folded up and buttoned or pinned to the shoulder straps; sometimes called an apron-front in modern writing about the Regency period.

apron-front *See* *apron.

artificial flowers Any imitation flower used for fashionable decoration; made from paper, *cambric, the inside of silkworm cocoons, silk fabrics, stamped *satin, lace, velvet, *whalebone or feathers; sometimes hand-painted to make them more realistic; occasionally perfumed with the appropriate scent, which increased the price.

ball dress (F) The ensemble worn at a ball. Gowns specifically for dancing were generally shorter at the hem, called dancing length. Longer gowns could be looped or pinned up to ensure the dancers did not trip on their own hems. Fashion plates for ball dress often show slimmer, shorter gowns than typical for normal *full dress. Lighter clothing for women was an advantage in a hot, crowded ballroom, which could be stifling.

'FULL OR DANCING DRESS . . . pink muslin or crape, with a long train . . . drawn [through] for dancing'

bandeau [band] An ornamental metal headband, fillet or narrow piece of fabric or ribbon, sometimes decorated, often supporting jewels, worn on or around a woman's head. Bandeaux could also be made of jewellery, which could then be worn separately, too.

John Downman, Maria Basevi, Mrs Isaac D'Israeli, *1805*

Barcelona [Barsalona] handkerchief A twilled silk handkerchief measuring around 20 to 28 inches (50–70 cm) square; plain, checked or with fancy patterns, and usually brightly coloured. Handkerchiefs of this kind were first manufactured in Spain, then in England. Women tied them around the neck and shoulders, pinned them up to create a turban, tied them cross-ways over the bosom and in a bow at the back, held hats and bonnets on with them tied under the chin, and used myriad other ways of fashioning the handkerchiefs.

basque skirt *See* *peplum.

bathing dress (F) Ensembles of clothing worn to bathe at the seaside or in natural springs at spa towns. Women wore high-necked voluminous *shifts with elbow- or full-length sleeves made from blue or white *flannel, *stuff, *calimanco or blue linen, worn with a linen or oiled silk *cap to cover the hair. Linen textiles were more often worn for spa-bathing, while woollen flannel and stuff textiles protected wearers from cold seas. When beaches were sex-segregated, some women bathed naked.

Thomas Rowlandson, 'Widow Ducker & her Nymphs' (detail) from Poetical Sketches of Scarborough, *1813*

bedgown An informal jacket or gown, usually short (above the knees) with loose sleeves, worn at home, or by working women, often over a petticoat or other gown. A kind of *morning dress. Also called a short gown or shortgown in Scotland during this period.

boa A long, slender stole or scarf, usually made of some fluffy material such as fur, swansdown or silk pile like *shag, in a range of tones matching natural fur. The word 'tippet' was quite interchangeable in fashion descriptions. *See* *stole, *tippet.

bodice [body] (1) Any part of a woman's dress or garment worn around the upper torso; the upper part of the gown, or the lining of that part. It could be separate, or have the skirt or *petticoat attached. The amount of décolletage a bodice revealed was described as low, three-quarter, full (to the collarbone), high (above the collarbone; *see* *high gown). (2) A quilted or boned undergarment such as a *corset, *jumps or *stays.

bonnet (1) A soft, brimless cap made of fabric, or knitted, often synonymous with *cap. (2) Structured women's headgear for outdoor wear, having a brim at the front and sides only, unlike a *hat; called *capote* in French. Brimmed bonnets were made of *willow, *chip, *Leghorn, *pasteboard, and many types of fabric. They would be plaited and sewn into shape or made in parts from a separate brim or *front attached to a solid or soft back (*cawl). It was tied under the chin with 'strings' or *ribbons, and trimmed with any combination of ribbons of all sorts and colours, *flowers, *cord, *gimp, *galloon, feathers, and more. Trimmings were often pinned rather than sewn on, for ease of changing them. Bonnet styles and their names were innumerable, reflecting battles, celebrities, aristocrats, literature, and other fashion novelties. All of the named variations found in period sources are too great to define here, but popular types included the French bonnet, *Oldenburg bonnet, *poke bonnet and *round bonnet. *See also* the entries under *headwear.

Unknown artist, miniature portrait of a woman in a straw bonnet, c.1800–5

boots (F) Footwear with a closed front, reaching to the ankle or just below the calf, worn during the day, for walking and in winter. Also called half-boots, as they were shorter than men's knee-high *boots (M), or 'high shoes'. Usually laced in front. Made of leather, including *kid, and sturdy textiles such as *jean or *nankeen. Those especially for walking were 'galoshed' with a leather lower half or front. Satin or silk half-boots did exist for evening wear, but were thought 'inappropriate' by fashion commentators.

Pair of woman's ankle boots, tan silk, lined with linen, leather heel and sole, 1804

bosom friend A bodice or insertion into a bodice to protect the bosom from cold or to increase its proportions. *See also* *Circassian corset.

Brandenburgs [Brandenburghs, Brandenbourgs] Twisted or looped braid ornamental trimmings, and sometimes button closures, copied from uniforms of military officers.

'A pelisse of pale pink sarsnet . . . ornamented with rich silk Brandenburgs trimmings'. 'Walking dress' (detail), June 1811

brisé fan A twentieth-century term for a form of folding fan constructed wholly from bladelike sticks usually made of bone, horn or ivory, frequently embellished by highly intricate carved or pierced designs in filigree or lace patterns and interlaced by a ribbon or thread. European fans of this type imitated Chinese wood or ivory examples made for export and imported by the East India Company. *See also* *fan.

busk A smooth, straight piece of wood or bone inserted into the front of a pair of *stays or a *corset between the breasts to separate them and to keep a straight centre line.

calash [ugly] A large, folding hood, made of silk or satin supported by hoops of cane or whalebone, and projecting beyond the face. It was designed to protect high headwear and hairstyles out of doors. A long loop of ribbon hanging from the front and held in the hand prevented the hood from blowing backwards. From the French, *calèche*: a lightweight carriage with a removable, collapsible hood.

Black silk (faded) calash with a pink lining, late 18th century

canezou (Fr.) A short, full, gathered *jacket garment reaching to the waist or above, with a peplum frill created by a drawstring, worn over a *bodice, with short, or later long, full sleeves, often made of a cotton or linen fabric such as *cambric or *muslin. Could be decorated. Could also be described as a *wrap or wrapper in English.

Charles Howard Hodges, Emma Jane Hodges, The Artist's Daughter, c.*1810*

cap A general term for any close-fitting headdress of soft material and structure, worn in informal domestic settings, especially in the morning, and ubiquitous for women; called *cornette* in French. Evening caps were made of higher quality and more decorative materials; the habitual wearing of caps in the evening, instead of dressed hair, denoted middle age. A woman's cap could also be worn out of doors, under a bonnet, or it could be a synonym for a brimless *bonnet. Fashion magazines present an innumerable range of fashionable varieties – more than can be presented here. *See also* *Mameluke cap, *mob cap.

James Lonsdale, Mrs Thomas Linley, c.*1815–20*

cape (F) An elbow-length cloak, or the attached circular addition(s) falling from under the collar of a cloak or coat and draping over the shoulders to provide extra warmth. *See* *tippet, *pelerine, *cloak.

capote *See* *bonnet.

Cardinal cloak [cardinal] A three-quarter- or ankle-length *cloak made from bright red wool, *worsted or *frieze fabric, with an attached hood, and sometimes a shoulder cape. Worn by women at all levels of British society. The shape and colour resembled a cardinal's robe.

John Constable, Portrait of Ann and Mary Constable: The Artist's Sisters, *1810–14*

carriage dress A type of *half-dress worn for visiting and in the afternoon, ostensibly suitable for wear in a carriage, and a degree more elaborate than *walking dress. Carriages were expensive to set up and maintain, and access to such a private vehicle was a luxury, even for gentlewomen, so the ensembles were not necessarily worn within a carriage. For long-distance coach travel, a sturdy *riding-habit was preferred.

'A bias corded muslin dress, a walking length'. 'Morning Carriage Dress', March 1811

cawl [caul] (1) The soft fabric back part of a bonnet, taking the place of a structured crown, and attached to the brim or front. (2) The fabric cover applied over a bonnet foundation.

chemise *See* *shift.

chemise gown A style of gown worn from the 1780s, thought of as resembling a *chemise; it was made of light, white cotton fabric, usually *muslin, with a low, round neck gathered on a drawstring, and it was cinched under the bust with a sash. It merged into the white muslin dresses popular from the mid-1790s onwards.

chemisette [chemisette front] (1) A tabard covering the upper part of the body and filling in the neck of a gown, often appearing like a false shirt front with a collar; it fastened with a drawstring at the waist or under the bust, made of linen, cotton, or the same fabric as the gown. The term appeared in the later Regency period; earlier, the garment might be called a collared *neck-handkerchief (referring to the way a woman's neck-handkerchief filled in the décolletage) or a *habit-shirt. (2) As 'chemisette front', a style of cutting a gown *bodice, open in front and gathered with a drawstring under the bust.

Circassian corset [Circassian vest, Circassian bodice] A type of fabric underbodice, *bosom friend or *corset, made to support the bust through shape, without any extra boning or cording for stiffness, buttoning, or lacing at the front. It was easier and quicker to put on and take off than laced *stays or corsets. The name comes from

Charles Ansell, 'The virgin shape warehouse', 1 September 1799

a short waistcoat perceived to be worn as part of the traditional dress of Circassians, a Northwest Caucasian ethnic group, and is documented under this name from at least 1799, despite claims of later dressmakers to have invented it.

cloak (F) (1) A loose outer garment, worn over other clothing for warmth and protection outside. It was like a *cape, gathered or cut in a semi-circle, fastening around the neck, and falling to the knees or lower – three-quarter or full length. At this time, it was more often called a *mantle, but could also be called a *wrapping cloak. Women's cloaks could additionally be made of light, decorative textiles such as printed cotton, silks, muslins, and the purely decorative lace, worn for style. (2) A long, rectangular garment like a shawl or scarf, usually a piece of silk or lace, commonly black, and trimmed with deep lace, usually machine-made, worn around the shoulders with the long ends clasped together at the front or crossing over. The ends reached to the hips or ground. This garment could be called a scarfed cloak.

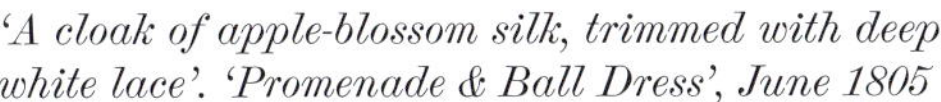
'A cloak of apple-blossom silk, trimmed with deep white lace'. 'Promenade & Ball Dress', June 1805

clock The shaping at the ankle of a stocking, tapering off up the leg; the clock was often knitted as an open net, in a decorative pattern, or embroidered with coloured silks or metallic threads.

clogs Wooden- or leather-soled overshoes, worn out of doors, to raise the wearer above dirt and wet ground. *See also* *pattens.

collar (F) Part of clothing going around the neck, at this time either a separate accessory made of *muslin, *cambric, *lawn, *lace and other fine cotton or linen fabrics, or attached to the neck of a *shirt, collared *neck-handkerchief, or *chemisette. Collars could be plain, like those of male shirts, or could be pleated (*see* *plait [T]), *quilled, cut in *Vandykes, embroidered, or have myriad other kinds of decorations. *See also* *ruff.

John Constable, Portrait of Mrs Edwards, *c.1818*

cornette (Fr.) A French word for an indoor *cap, tied under the chin. Appears in fashion commentary after 1815.

corset [corsette] (1) A close-fitting, soft undergarment, worn to support the breasts and shape the silhouette. In the 1790s corsets were originally a new garment, shorter and lighter than stiffly boned *stays, made from fabric and using *cording or *whalebone for shape. From the early nineteenth century onwards the terms 'stays' and 'corset' began to converge, as corsets were more commonly worn, became longer, and had more boning in them. (2) In fashion, a kind of sleeveless, decorative waistcoat or bolero, worn over, and usually contrasting with, the gown. Sometimes called a 'French body', a literal translation of 'corset' ('little body').

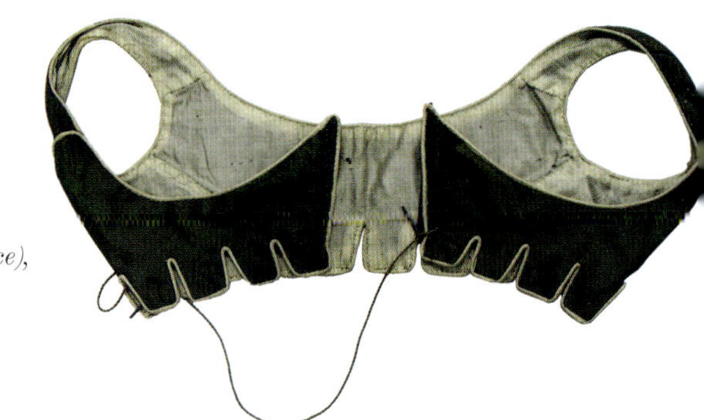

Olive green silk external corset (bodice), corded with white silk, c.1800–20

cottage cloak A cloak gathered at or about the shoulders to create fullness, as in the *Cardinal cloak.

cottage hat [cottage bonnet] A straw or *chip hat, or bonnet tied with a ribbon to bring the brim down by the ears. Similar to a *gipsy hat.

'Cottage bonnet of yellow twilled sarsnet'. 'Morning Dress' (detail), 1 October 1812

court dress (F) The highest, most formal version of *full dress fulfilling the regulations for appearing at court, subject to strict convention. Women were required to wear an open gown over a *petticoat, full ruffles on the sleeves usually made from fine lace or *blonde, and *lappets (streamers attached to the head-dress) made of the same, or black lace. Queen Charlotte also insisted on retaining the archaic eighteenth-century hoop petticoats (but no other earlier styles) as an obligatory part of court dress, even as waistlines rose; therefore, women's broad 'hips' started at their ribcage until George IV dispensed with hoops early in his reign. Women's finest jewels (especially *brilliants) were also expected in court dress. An 1809 guide explained more of the details: 'of late, it has been more the fashion to have the petticoat,

'Her Royal Highness the Princess of Wales in her Court Dress on the 4. of June 1807, as authentically taken from the real dress made by Mrs. Webb of Pall Mall'

both the drapery and the under part, of the same colour as the gown; but a coloured drapery over a white petticoat prevailed for many years, and the drapery was even often of a different colour from the gown. Velvet, sattin [*sic*], silk, crape, and gause [*sic*; gauze], are the only materials allowed for ladies' court dresses. . . . Court dresses are trimmed, and often embroidered with gold and silver; and artificial flowers are much used for ornamenting the petticoat. Feathers are not reckoned a necessary part of a court dress; but young ladies very seldom go without them, and they are supposed to be under dressed if they do.'[10]

curricle cloak A type of *cloak, half- or three-quarter length, shaped at the waist, the sides sloping off from the front.

curricle robe [curicle robe, curricle vest] A short, open *robe or *tunic, as curricles were light, two-wheeled, open carriages with shorter sides.

'The Demi Habillement, or Curicle Robe, with worked border', July 1798

dinner dress A type of *half-dress, one degree of formality below *full dress, made of silk, muslins, light wools such as *merino and quality *worsteds, and other fabrics tending more opaque. At minimum, one 'dressed' for dinner, even with family or friends, but, for home dinners, *walking or promenade dress was acceptable.

divorce [divorce corset] A style of *corset with a piece of triangular steel or iron, curved on each side, set in the middle as a *busk to separate the breasts.

douillette [donnillette] (Fr.) An outer coat or *pelisse with a layer of *wadding or other padding inside for added warmth.

Wadded silk satin douillette, c.1820

drawers (F)
Underwear trousers made of linen, cotton, knitted silk, or woollen fabrics; knee-, calf- or ankle-length when worn by a woman under a gown, although more often referred to as pantaloons (F) when reaching below the knee.

Pair of white cotton drawers for a female doll, early 19th century

dress (F) (1) A shorthand for the more formal *full dress or *evening dress. (2) A woman's main garment, slowly being used in place of *gown in this period, more in the 1810s. (3) A whole ensemble, such as *walking dress or *morning dress.

dressing gown (F) A knee- to ankle-length robe worn over *nightgowns in private domestic settings before dressing for the day, when ill, or when resting. Made of white cotton, linen, muslin, wool flannel, and other washable textiles. Some morning gowns were in the form of an open robe that functioned as a dressing gown. Also called a wrapping-gown. More informal than the male *dressing-gown.

empire line, empire dress A twentieth-century name for the defining Regency style of high-waisted dresses, coined in 1907 when French designers started placing the waistline under the bust again and called the style 'Directoire' or 'Empire' after the post-French Revolution Directory period (1795–9) or Napoleon's First Empire (1804–15) . The phrase was never used in the historical period and is anachronistic when describing actual Regency gowns.

epaulette [epaulette sleeve] A decorative separate upper sleeve, often decorated with puffs, or historically inspired panes (bands of fabric). Often called a mancheron from the mid-1810s.

Epaulette sleeve of a cotton jacket, 1815

evening dress (F) A form of *dress or *full dress, sometimes interchangeable with these terms, comprising clothing and accessories suitable only for evening events (*cf.* *morning dress). General evening dress could be slightly less formal than *full dress, but still fell into the *dress category. Colours were recommended to be chosen to look good by candlelight.

Unknown artist,
Portrait of a Lady, c.*1815–20*

fan A rigid or folding handheld device used to stir the air and create a breeze. Folding fans comprise sticks (the outer two are called 'guards') made of wood, bone, horn, tortoiseshell or ivory; often decorated, gilded, carved or pierced; pinned or riveted together at the end; held together by a curved 'leaf' of paper, silk or sometimes lace, which unfurled to display a pattern or decorative scene. Smaller fans, sometimes called 'opera' size, were most popular. *See also* *brisé fan.

Ivory fan with green silk ribbon, c.1815–20

fan parasol A *parasol with a hinged stick so that the shade could provide either vertical or horizontal protection from the sun.

fichu A finished square or triangle of light linen or cotton, worn around a woman's neck, shoulders and chest for warmth and protection; it could be tucked into the gown or tied at the front. French-originating word, increasingly used to describe a *neckerchief, especially from the 1810s.

flowers Real and *artificial flowers were worn in the hair and at the bosom to ornament fashionable dress, especially in the evenings.

French bonnet A more common term for the *Oldenburg bonnet with a very high crown and a wide brim that hid the face, popular in France and contrasting with less voluminous English-style bonnet variations after the end of the Napoleonic Wars.

'French straw bonnet . . . trimmed . . . with a narrow quilling of net lace'. 'Promenade Dress' (detail), October 1814

frock A gown with bodice and skirt in one without a waist seam, or one that fastens at the back with ties, before back fastening became general in fashion.

front The brim or *peak of a *bonnet, as distinct from the *cawl. *See also* *front (HB).

full dress [dress] (F) An ensemble or a mode of dress appropriate for formal or public occasions in the afternoon or later, such as *ball dress, *court dress, *evening dress, or dress worn to the opera or formal dinners (*cf.* *half-dress). For women this was most often a *gown made of *muslin, *satin and other silks, *gauze, white or coloured *crape, or other high-quality, expensive or light textiles, especially those with metallic decorations that absorbed or reflected light; frequently white; frequently with elaborate embroidery and *trimmings, especially handmade *lace; necklines were low and displayed the bosom, and often shoulder blades; arms could be bare above the elbow. Contemporary commentators frequently alluded to how 'undressed' full dress was. Long sleeves started to become acceptable in full dress from the early 1810s. Worn with *slippers of white *kid or satin, the latter often embroidered. Headdresses often included feathers.

'A white satin slip under a gown of spotted net, both trimmed with blonde lace'. 'Full Dress', January 1817

gaiters (F) Leg coverings made of leather, cotton, linen, *fustian, *drill, *kerseymere or wool, extending from the ankle to the front of the foot, and fastened with buttons, or straps and buckles down the outer side. They added warmth to the feet and legs, and protection from dirt. Similar to the male *half-gaiters.

galosh (1) In the upper of a shoe, a piece of leather running all round the shoe and attached to the sole; it was made of stouter material than the rest of the body of the shoe and protected the foot from cold and wet. (2) In later use, a protective overshoe made of impermeable material. In the Regency, 'galoshes' of this kind were unknown, and other types of outer footwear were worn to protect the shoes from dirt and wet (*see* *clogs, *pattens). Occasionally spelled as calash, not to be confused with the *calash hood.

garter A long woven band, *ribbon, or other textile strap, usually in a pair, used to secure women's *stockings by tying below the knee (a slightly firmer grip) or above it around the thigh. If a woman's garter was on view, she was considered indecently exposed.

Pair of knitted white cotton garters, possibly worn for a wedding, 1798

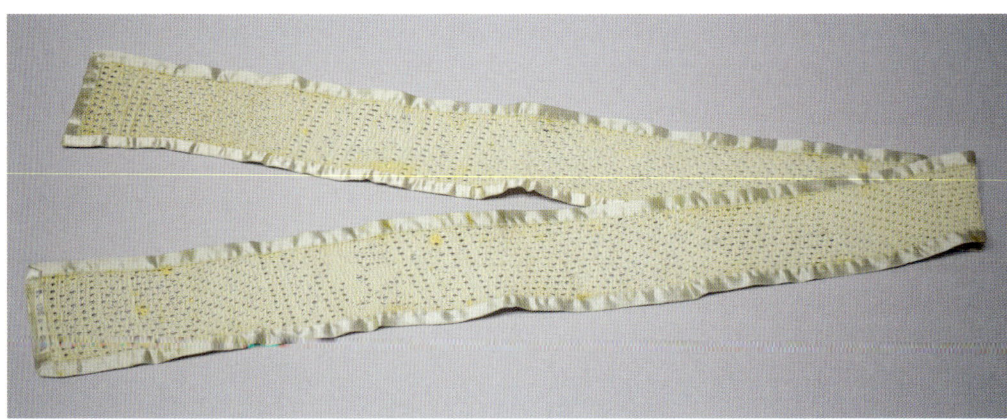

gipsy [gipsey, gypsy] hat A large-brimmed, circular straw hat, held on by a wide ribbon or sash running over the top of the hat and tied under the chin. Similar to a *cottage hat.

'A large gipsy hat of straw, or imperial chip, tied across the crown with a silk handkerchief'. 'Fashionable Spring Walking Dresses' (detail), 1 June 1808

girdle Another word for belt.

gloves (F) A covering for the whole of the hand, usually with individual fingers. Fingerless gloves are *mittens. Made from light, thin, flexible materials, especially leathers such as *beaver (4), *buff, doeskin, *chamois, *chicken-skin, *kid and *lambskin; and textiles including knitted or woven cotton, silk, *jean, *nankeen, *worsted, wool and linen, sometimes cut on the bias for greater elasticity. Glove leathers were cured with alum instead of tanning, which made them softer and more pliable. *Full dress gloves for evening wear were long, just below or above the elbow, often held up by a ribbon tied around the arm, but having the long glove pushed down onto the forearms was also acceptable. Short, wrist-length gloves for daywear were also called *habit gloves. The only acceptable colours for *full dress gloves were white or a buff tan, but coloured versions for *morning dress and *half-dress were widely available, if considered less genteel, and usually made of dyed kid. French gloves were the finest quality, but import restrictions frequently made them unavailable. *See also* *Limerick gloves, *York tans.

Woman's long suede gloves printed with decorative motifs, c.1820

gown The general word for the main garment women wore, in public or private, fitted to the upper body, with the length draping to the lower legs or floor. The term was gradually overtaken colloquially by 'dress' in this period, except in describing formal dresses of particular elegance. *See also* *bedgown, *bodice, *chemise gown, *dressing gown, *frock, *high gown, *long gown, *morning gown, *nightgown, *open gown, *round gown, *short gown, *wrapping gown.

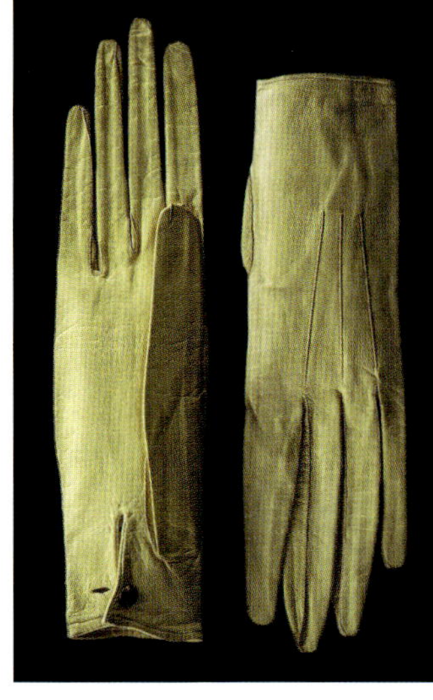

habit *See* *riding-habit.

habit gloves Short, wrist-length *gloves, originally worn with long-sleeved *riding-habit jackets; contrasting with long elbow-length evening gloves. Made from silk, cotton, and various kinds of leather.

Pair of yellow wrist-length kid leather habit gloves, c.1820

habit-shirt A kind of *shirt originally worn under a waistcoat or jacket as part of a riding ensemble (hence the name 'habit'), sometimes used to refer to any female shirt, to distinguish it from the male shirt, although women's were generally much shorter, coming to the bottom of the ribs, or top of the hips. *See also* *shirt.

Linen habit-shirt, c.1800

half-boot (F) *See* *boots.

half-dress A semi-formal ensemble or a mode of dress in between *undress and *full dress, appropriate for public events, such as daytime functions or informal evening gatherings, and often with slightly shorter hems, for mobility. *Afternoon, *carriage, *opera, *promenade, *seaside and *walking dress were all considered half-dress. In contemporary personal writings, the dress concerns that people most communicate are about the suitability of ensembles for *evening dress, and for *walking and *carriage dress, so 'half' is more usually implied by contrast with 'full' dress than used as a specific term. The phrase by the anonymous author of *Dress and Address*, 'the intermediate order of dress', best summarises the clothing between morning and full dress.

'Morning Promenade & Opera Dresses', March 1813

half-handkerchief *See* *handkerchief.

half-robe [half-gown] A low-necked, thigh-length tunic worn over a *round gown. *See* *curricle robe, *robe.

handkerchief (F) 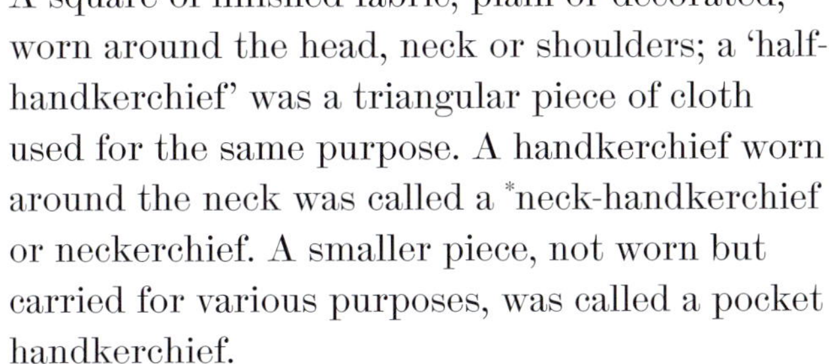
A square of finished fabric, plain or decorated, worn around the head, neck or shoulders; a 'half-handkerchief' was a triangular piece of cloth used for the same purpose. A handkerchief worn around the neck was called a *neck-handkerchief or neckerchief. A smaller piece, not worn but carried for various purposes, was called a pocket handkerchief.

'Lilac silk handkerchief [on the hat and] round the shoulders, crossed in front and fastened with a gold pin', June 1802

handkerchief-sash A long, wide, triangular or rectangular piece of light material, fringed at the edges like a handkerchief, used as a sash for tying over *gowns.

hat (F) (1) An article of *headwear made by a hatter, usually of wool or fur, manipulated and shaped on moulds; or of straw, by milliners or straw hatters. (2) A synonym for any kind of headwear, usually with a brim.

headwear Any type of *bonnet, *cap or *hat. *See* *calash, **capote*, *cottage hat, *French bonnet, *gipsy hat, *jockey hat, *Mameluke cap, *Mary Stuart hat, *Minerva hat, *mob cap, *nightcap, *poke bonnet, *riding hat, *riding-hood, *round bonnet, *trencher hat, *turban. Hats were made by hatters; bonnets and caps by milliners and dressmakers.

high back A *gown with a bodice neckline finishing above the shoulder blades at the back. *Cf.* *low back.

high gown *Morning dress with a high neckline, to or past the collarbone.

home costume A term used from the 1810s for *undress or *morning dress worn at home during the day.

indispensable *See* *ridicule.

jacket (F) (1) Any short, close-fitting outer coat, sometimes but not always called a *spencer. For women, such a jacket was waist-length, in accordance with the fashionable waistline. (2) A long-sleeved separate bodice with a matching *petticoat that together made a dress.

'Jacket of Venetian lake-coloured satin . . . trimmed with black lace', March 1800

'London Head Dresses, May, 1800'

1
2
3
4
5
6
9

jockey hat [jockey bonnet] Headwear inspired by or resembling the caps worn by jockeys, with a small front brim.

'Taken from the Walking Dresses in Kensington Garden', 1 June 1806

jumps [bodies] A soft, unboned under-bodice, worn at home by women instead of *stays; jumps were often padded or quilted, with a *stomacher to fill the gap where they were laced at the front. *See also* *bodice (2), *waistcoat (2).

kerchief *See* *handkerchief.

latchets The pair of long tabs or straps extending from the top front of a shoe, which overlap and pass through the buckle to fasten closed, or tie together with a lace or 'string'.

Limerick gloves Gloves made of *chicken-skin – a thin, bright yellow suede from the skins of unborn calves, kids or lambs, named for Limerick in Ireland, where such gloves were first made. They were prized for their extreme fineness and elasticity. The best quality were so fine they could be pulled through a ring or were sold folded up in a walnut shell. 'The Limerick Gloves', a story by Maria Edgeworth (1768–1849) published in 1804, helped to popularise them.

Elbow-length Limerick gloves, made of 'chicken-skin' leather, early 19th century

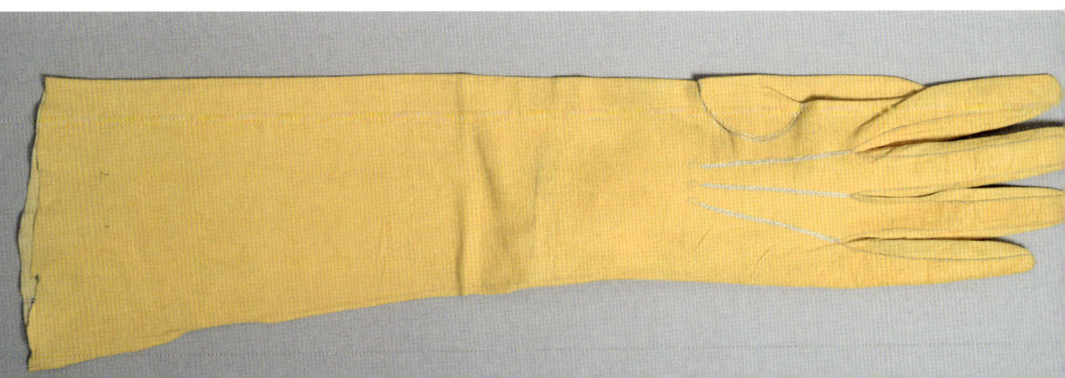

list shoes [list slippers] Soft, thick, warm footwear for both sexes made from *list, the selvedges of woollen textiles cut off by weavers and clothworkers and re-woven into a new textile, lined with *baize. List footwear was worn as *undress indoors, in carriages, by the sick and by those who cared for them, as the soft soles made no noise. They could also become overshoes when worn over thin fashion *slippers.

long gown One with a train, beyond ankle-length.

long purse *See* *purse.

long stays [long corset] *See* *stays.

low back A *gown with a bodice neckline finishing over or below the shoulder blades at the back. *Cf.* *high back.

Mameluke cap An evening turban with a crescent at the centre front, inspired by mamluks, a military knightly class comprising non-Arab slave-soldiers and freed slaves across Muslim Mediterranean-bordering areas, especially Egypt. Spelling variations include mamaluke, mameluk, mameluke, mamlouk, mamluke, mamluq and marmeluke.

mancheron [à *la mancheron*] (Fr. 'plough handle') *See* *epaulette.

mantelet A short, small, or less full *cloak or *mantle. From the French.

mantle A loose, sleeveless, enveloping outer garment, of variable length, for outdoor wear. *See also* *cloak.

'A light sky-blue mantle, lined with pale buff'. 'Morning Walking Dress', 1 July 1810

Mary Stuart hat [Mary Stuart cap, Marie Stuart cap] Headwear dipping to a peak at the centre front, inspired by stage costumes for and depictions of the sixteenth-century Mary Stuart, Queen of Scots, whose popularity as a tragic, romantic cultural figure at the time was fuelled by many histories, poems, plays, operas and literary fiction narratives about her.

Minerva hat [Minerva bonnet] Any helmet-shaped hat with a feather, named for the Roman goddess of war.

miser's purse *See* *purse.

mittens [mitts] Fingerless gloves that covered the arm, worn for warmth while allowing dexterity; they were often made of lightweight, openwork or knitted fabrics.

mob cap A large, soft, indoor *cap of lightweight linen or cotton, consisting of a rounded *cawl with a ruffled brim, and drawn in with strings that tied under the chin; it covered most of the hair.

John Russell, Mrs Robert Shurlock Sr (Ann Manwaring), *wearing a mob cap, 1801*

morning dress (F) An *undress ensemble or a mode of dress for informal daywear at home or outdoors in the hours before the afternoon. For women, indoor morning dress usually consisted of a high-cut, long-sleeved *round gown or *morning gown; when layered with a bonnet and outer garment, such as a *pelisse, morning dress was also appropriate for walking, shopping, running errands and making informal visits. Sometimes called negligee. (*Cf.* *evening dress.) *See also* *bedgown, *high gown, *home costume, *morning gown, *wrap.

Rolinda Sharples, The Artist and her Mother, *both wearing morning dress, 1816*

morning gown (F) A gown worn as *morning dress at home throughout the day before changing for dinner, made of white or printed cotton or linen fabrics of various weights or light *worsted and worsted-blend materials, such as *stuff and *bombazine, and slightly looser in fit than *half-dress or *full dress garments, often with a high collar (*high gown) and long sleeves. If the gown was white, as many were, the decoration would often be white embroidery or lace, or trimmings made of the same or other white fabric, such as tucks and frills, creating visual interest without colour.

High-necked muslin morning gown, c.1817

mourning dress (F) Black and sombre-coloured clothing and accessories worn as a public display of grief and mourning for a death in the family, or in the extended royal family. The closeness of the relationship determined the length and degree of mourning dress. Full mourning required black clothes in dull, non-shiny textiles, primarily *bombazine and *crape; and *chamois leather for gloves and shoes. While there were social conventions about length of time and depth of mourning in dress, they were defined as much by their flouting as their observance.

Louis Vaslet, 'Scene II', The Spoiled Child *(detail), c.1802*

muff A cylindrical or flat tube, made from fur, feathers or fabric, into each end of which the hands were inserted for warmth. Muffs were padded within, and often had one or more small internal pockets.

Afternoon dress, 'long black bear opera-tippet and muff', January 1801

muffetees [muffatees, muftees] Very short *mittens or small wrist muffs, often knitted; they were worn for warmth or to protect *shirt cuffs.

neckerchief *See* *neck-handkerchief.

neck-handkerchief [neckerchief, double handkerchief] (F) A square, finished piece of cloth, worn around the neck, or over the shoulders and décolletage. Neckerchiefs were made in a huge variety of plain, printed or woven coloured cottons and silks. All handkerchiefs of the larger sort tended to take the width of the fabric off the roll as their measure. A yard square (36 in./91 cm) was common, usually made of fine linen or cotton textiles such as *muslin, *cambric and *lawn. A collared neck-handkerchief was another term for the garment now usually called a *chemisette. *See also* *fichu, *handkerchief.

negligee [negligé, negligée] *See* *undress, *morning dress.

nightcap [night bonnet] (F) A close-fitting cap, usually tying underneath the chin, worn in bed at night for warmth and to stop women's long hair tangling. Generally made of linen or cotton fabrics including *muslin, and could be decorated with lace, embroidery, frills, gathering and other decoration. The same cap pattern could be used for a day or night item, depending on the quality of the fabric chosen.

Isaac Cruikshank, The Cuckold Departs for the Hunt *(detail), c.1800, depicting a nightcap and nightgown*

nightgown [night chemise] (F) A loose gown worn in bed to sleep in, usually made of *calico or linen fabric. Similar to a *shift, but ankle-length. Fancier versions could be made of muslin or gauze, and could be decoratively trimmed. *See* image for *nightcap.

nosegay A small bouquet of real flowers, preferably fragrant ones, worn as adornment on the bodice of a gown.

Oldenburg bonnet A style of bonnet worn by the Grand Duchess of Oldenburg (1788–1819), with a very high crown and a wide brim that hid the face; it was popular throughout Europe after the duchess's tour of 1814. It was particularly popular in France, and the style was more often called a *French bonnet.

open gown A *gown with a skirt that opened down the centre front.

opera dress A kind of *evening or *full dress.

painted border A brief fashion for painting birds, flowers, or other natural elements on the hems of *full dress gowns, made from white *crape, *tiffany, *muslin or *velvet.

pantalets [pantalettes] *See* *pantaloons.

pantaloons [pantalet(te)s, trowsers] (F) Linen or cotton calf- or ankle-length loose *drawers, worn under the skirt and sometimes visible below it, especially when worn with a shorter *frock, and often with decorative pin tucks, embroidery or lace on the hems. The legs were joined at the waistband, but were open over the crotch and some way down the upper leg, for convenience.

Pair of cotton pantaloons, worn by Louisa Dexter, 1802–20

parasol [parasole] A kind of spoked, foldable umbrella used as protection from the sun. They provided adjustable shade for the upper body, while a bonnet or hat brim shielded the face. The sticks were made of wood, metal or bone, and were often collapsible. The covers were made of linen or silk, in every colour, often green like umbrellas, and sometimes decorated and trimmed at the edges with fringing. When folded, parasols were generally held by a wrist loop at the fabric or ferrule end, instead of the handle. *See also* *fan parasol.

'Parasol purple shot, and fringed with amber [at back], pink shot with brown', November 1809

pattens Overshoe or *clog, consisting of a wooden sole attached to a tall metal ring, held on the foot by leather straps. Pattens were worn over normal shoes when walking outside, to raise the wearer above dirt and wet ground. They were practical but not fashionable footwear.

Pair of wood and leather pattens with a raised iron circle, early 19th century

peak The *front or brim of a bonnet, as distinct from the *cawl.

pelerine A small *mantle or *cape, made of lace, silk or fur, with the lower edges curving to meet at a point at the front. French for 'cape'. Similar to a *tippet, and sometimes the names are used as equivalents in fashion plates. The evolution is made clear in an 1811 reference to 'tippets *à-la-pelerine*'.[11]

pelisse [pelice, pellice, pelisse-greatcoat] (F) A coat-dress, made from many kinds of material, from light *muslin to thick wool; lined or unlined. It could be of any length from the knee to the ankle, and have any of various styles of collar, cape and sleeves, which were almost always long; it was usually somewhat fitted, to follow the form of the *gown worn underneath. Could be cut with a waist seam, or in continuous pieces from shoulder to hem. Tapes or *ribbons were attached at the centre back inside to tie around the waist to keep the pelisse in place during wear, before fastening it with buttons, ties or *Brandenburgs, or by pinning the front edges together.

'A pelisse of . . . lilac figured sarsnet . . . short [enough] to show the flounce of the morning dress', September 1812

peplum [basque skirt] A flared or gathered width of fabric forming the part of a woman's *jacket that hung below the waist.

petticoat (1) Any skirt, whether visible or worn underneath a gown or other petticoats; in this sense, sometimes abbreviated to 'coat'. (2) The skirt of a dress, as distinct from the bodice, with which it could be coloured to match or contrast. (3) A skirted garment with its own bodice – usually sleeveless – to hold it up, worn under a gown (especially when made of transparent fabric), or, for informal wear, over a *shirt. *See also* *slip.

Cotton petticoat with a lace frill and hand-embroidered whitework insertion, 1810–20

pinafore [pin-a-fore] (1) An *apron that covered the chest, so called because it originated from a piece of fabric pinned to the front of the gown or shirt. (2) A sleeveless protective garment with a skirt, fastening at the back.

plait The Regency spelling of 'pleat', a straight fold in fabric. *Cf.* *plait (T and HB).

pocket (F) (1) A separate detached bag or pouch worn by women, usually under their skirts, either above or below their *petticoats, and accessed through slits in the side seams of the outer garment. Pockets were attached, either singly or in pairs, to a tape that was tied around the waist. They were considered unfashionable by the later Regency, but they never completely disappeared in favour of small bags such as *ridicules. (2) A small pocket or *fob set into the waist seam.

pocket handkerchief *See* *handkerchief.

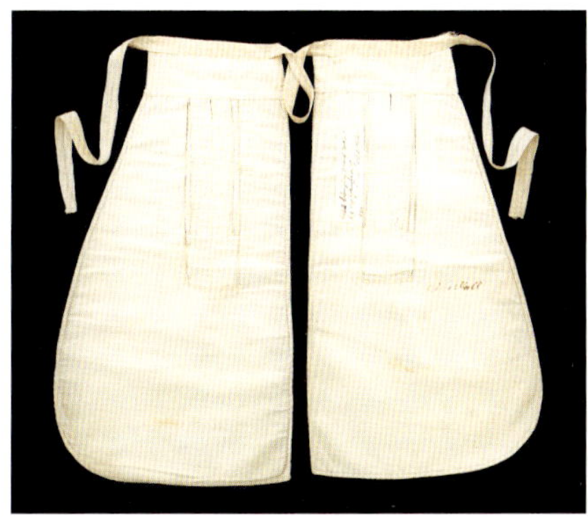

Pocket slit in a morning dress, white openwork cotton, 1815–18

Pair of cotton pockets, worn by Ann Isabel Hale, 1820

poke bonnet A bonnet with a crown fitting close to the head, and a long brim, often cylindrical in shape, extending horizontally out over the face. The deep front brim provided weather protection, though it could be lengthened for fashion, as in the poke bonnets that satirists delighted in representing as two feet (60 cm) long.

Poke bonnet of green silk, chenille braid and cord, lined in pink silk, 1806–9

promenade dress *See* *walking dress.

pumps (F) Flat, light, close-fitting dancing or evening shoes with no rand (strip of leather between the sole and the upper), made as turn shoes (sewn inside out, then 'turned' the right way round), open over the instep or with a strap, and often laced with ribbons over the instep and ankle.

Evening white satin pump, with two silk ankle straps, lined with cotton, c.1815

purse Any small pouch or bag for carrying money, made of textile or leather. The popular long, tubular purse with an access slit in the centre, closed with two metal slider rings, was known as a miser's, long, stocking, ring or string purse. Such purses were often crocheted, netted or knitted, and might be decorated with beads. *See also* *ridicule.

Netted silk purse with cut steel beads, chain, handles and slider, early 19th century

Queen Elizabeth ruff [Queen Elizabeth collar] *See* *ruff.

redingote A long, single- or double-breasted and full-skirted coat, with a prominent collar and a fitted body, worn outdoors, for riding, or when travelling. The word is a French corruption of 'riding-coat', borrowed back into English, and was not frequently used. *Great coat or *pelisse were more usual terms, depending on the garment's cut.

rand A strip of leather between the sole and the upper to which the sole was sewn.

reticule *See* *ridicule.

ridicule [reticule, indispensable] A small, round, square or lozenge-shaped handbag, made of soft materials including everything from *muslin to velvet, knitted or netted. It was often embellished with embroidery or beading, and was drawn closed and suspended from the hand or arm by a loop of ribbon. Usually somewhat larger than a purse.

'Ridicule or hand-pocket', November 1799

riding-habit [habit] A woman's garment of woollen cloth, modelled on the male riding ensemble. Made by a tailor used to manipulating wool textiles, it consisted of a waistcoat (optional), a fitted, double-breasted jacket, and a long skirt, usually with a train. The jacket had long sleeves and often a short *peplum or basque skirt, with collar, cuffs and buttons echoing men's dress. Fabric preferences varied with fashion and season, using lighter shades in lighter materials, such as *nankeen, during summer. It was also worn for occasions other than riding, including for different sporting activities, informal daywear and travel, and was often simply called a 'habit'. This is the origin of the *habit-shirt, worn underneath the jacket, and *habit gloves, wrist-length to fit a habit's long sleeves.

'Riding habits of the most fashionable colours, corbeau or olive', December 1798

riding hat (1) Any hat worn while riding, accessorising a *riding-habit. (2) A particular fashionable silhouette, inspired by the military shako, especially the version worn with Hussar uniforms. It resembled a top hat in the height and cylindrical shape of the crown, with little or no brim.

'Black beaver hat, trimmed with a purple velvet ribband', June 1795

riding-hood A large, detached hood worn by women to protect from the elements while horse riding.

ring purse *See* *purse.

robe [half-robe, half-gown] (1) An evening gown or over-garment open in front to display a decorative petticoat, and with a train behind. A 'half-robe' or 'half-gown' was a low-necked, thigh-length tunic worn over a gown. (2) Any loose garment (as in the modern sense).

'SUMMER WALKING DRESSES . . . Fig. 2 . . . Short robe . . . Fig. 3 . . . Short robe of lilac muslin', June 1799

roll A cylindrical or crescent-shaped padded accessory tied under the top of the skirt at the back, to increase the volume slightly when that was in fashion.

rosette [rose, roset] A detachable trimming for evening shoes, made from ribbon, gold or silver-gilt metal or textiles, or bugle beads.

round bonnet A bonnet with a flared, open brim.

round gown A gown with bodice and skirt in one; the skirt was closed all round, and not open in front to expose the petticoat. It emerged in the 1790s and continued to be worn through this period.

Deep rose pink silk round gown, c.1797–1805

ruff [Queen Elizabeth ruff, Queen Elizabeth collar] A highly frilled *collar, with one to four layers of linen, cotton, lace or gauze frills, resembling sixteenth-century ruffs.

sandals Slippers or shoes that tied or laced up over the instep to the ankle and sometimes higher, or that had a pattern on the vamp imitating lacing.

Unknown artist, 'The Graces Comparing Sandals', 1 May 1798

scarfed cloak *See* *cloak.

seaside dress A kind of lighter *half-dress or *walking dress for wearing at the seaside, with a slightly shorter hem.

shawl A rectangular or square piece of any textile, including silk, linen, *muslin, wool and *cashmere, used as a covering for the shoulders, upper arms and torso, and sometimes worn over the head. The garment originally came from India and was predominantly a male garment. Most prized and expensive were Kashmiri shawls of light, warm cashmere. Europeans in India adopted the local fashion and brought back valuable shawls as presents and souvenirs. These shawls were originally woven in pairs and worn with wrong sides together, so no construction showed. Joining two squares together end to end made the long shawl in the form of a rectangle. These could be attached at the shoulders to form a 'flowing train', and were also made into *gowns. European manufacturers' cheap copies soon flooded the market, fulfilling the demand but decreasing the fashionability by making shawls common.

Woollen shawl with boteh motifs handwoven in Kashmir, c.1820

shift A woman's knee-length undergarment of washable plain linen or (usually after *c*.1820) cotton, worn next to the skin to protect outer clothing, and always worn underneath *corsets and *stays to protect the body from rubbing, and to keep the supportive garments clean. A shift was also called by the older word 'smock', and in the Regency period came to be called a 'chemise'. The two words were used interchangeably. Shifts had a wide, round or rectangular neckline as the gown demanded. The shift reached the knees, with long side gussets, and had short, straight sleeves no longer than the elbow. A gathered *muslin frill could be sewn around the neckline and removed during laundering.

Linen shift, 1810s

shirt [habit-shirt] (F) A woman's linen or cotton garment, usually with long sleeves like a man's shirt, or sleeveless; worn under a low-necked *gown, or under a *petticoat with a sleeveless *bodice for informal wear at home; it might also be made of or trimmed with *cambric, *muslin, lace or *net, and often had ruffles at neck and wrists. A *habit-shirt, with or without sleeves, was worn under a waistcoat or jacket as part of a *riding-habit ensemble, though the name could be interchangeable with 'shirt'. A sleeveless form of shirt could be called a *shirt handkerchief, shirt-kerchief, collared neckerchief and, later, a *chemisette. *See also* *shirt handkerchief and *chemisette.

shirt handkerchief A triangular *neckerchief closing or buttoning down the front like a *shirt, with or without a collar, could be called a shirt-kerchief, collared neckerchief or *chemisette.

Shirt handkerchief with gathered collar of bobbin net and lace, c.1820

shoes (1) A general term for footwear. (2) Footwear made with a welted rand (a strip of leather between the sole and the upper to which the sole was sewn), and adjustable tied straps to hold it on the foot, differing from a *slipper which was made to the shape of the foot and slipped onto it. The shaped higher heels of women's shoes diminished during the 1790s and had disappeared into a small wedge or lift (one piece of sole leather) by about 1800. Shoes ended in mainly pointed toes, alongside some oval shapes, which became generally rounder through the 1800–10s, evolving into a squarer toe by the 1820s. Shoes were generally made on 'straight' lasts (the wooden form), with no left and right – which were created through use. Right and left or 'crooked' lasts did exist but were not yet popular and were used mainly for men's shoes. *See also* *boots, *clogs, *pumps, *sandals, *slippers.

Pair of woman's slippers made from black leather, 1790–1810

short gown One without a train; ankle-length.

short stays *See* *stays.

sleeves Detachable long sleeves made separately from a *gown, either of matching fabric or of decorative or plain linen, cotton and silk fabrics, woven or knitted, then tied with a drawstring or pinned to the armhole underneath short sleeves to add warmth, to make the gown more versatile in style, to transition between *morning and *evening dress, or to denote *mourning, in the case of *crape sleeves.

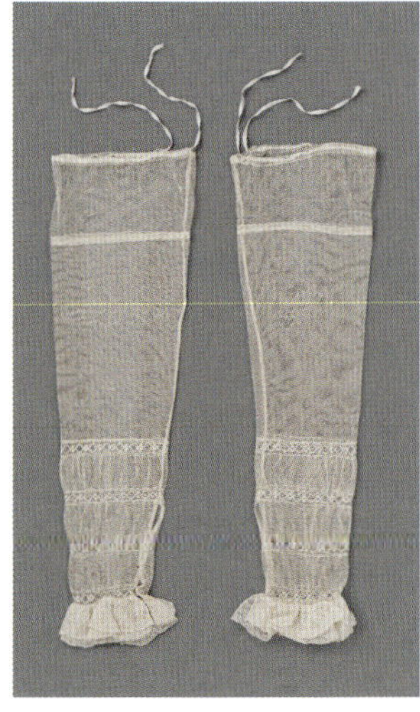

Pair of separate tie-on bobbin net sleeves with Mechlin lace cuffs, c.1815–20

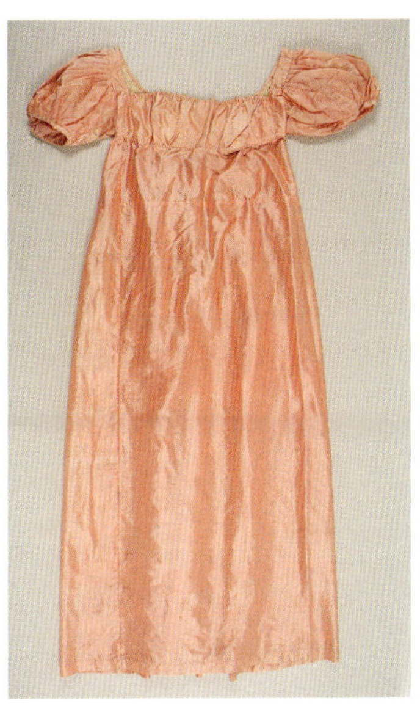

slip (F) A plain silk or *satin undergown or petticoat, white or coloured, worn under a transparent *muslin, *net or *gauze gown. The colour of the slip changed the colour of the outer gown, as it was seen through the fabric.

Pink silk slip, 1815–20

slippers (F) A type of *shoe with a lower throat (the top front line of a shoe), allowing the foot to slip in without requiring a pair of *latchets, or a strap fastened with a buckle to close it, although evening slippers could be tied on with ribbons to ensure they stayed on the foot.

smock A woman's undergarment of linen or (later) cotton, worn next to the skin (*see* *shift).

spencer [spenser, spinser] (F) A short, close-fitting jacket without tails; the term is probably more common in modern usage than it was at the time. Originally worn by men over a longer coat, the spencer then became popular with women and remained so throughout the Regency. The woman's spencer followed the form of the gown bodice over which it was worn. Fashion histories often attribute the short half-coat's invention to George Spencer, 4th Duke of Marlborough (1739–1817); however, the earliest references in periodicals of around 1795 name the originator as his brother Charles (1740–1820), who 'betted some friends, that he could sport a fashion, the most useless and ridiculous that could be conceived, and that it should . . . be universally adopted'.[12]

Yellow silk spencer jacket, lined with cotton, 1810–14

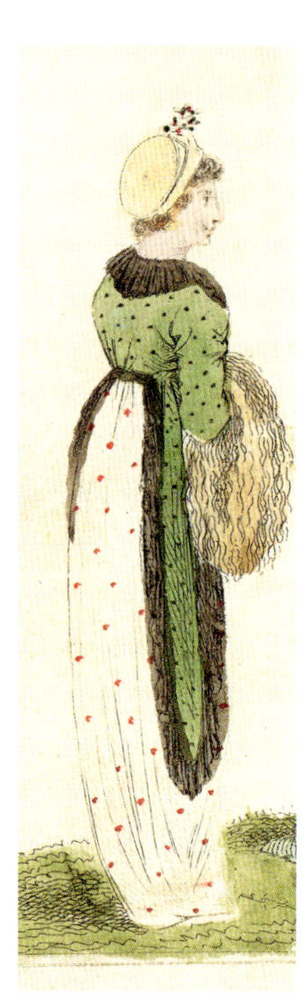

spencer cloak [spencer-cloak, Spencer mode cloak] *Cloak in the sense of the long, rectangular garment like a shawl or scarf, with the addition of short sleeves, and a gathering under the bust.

Spencer cloak of green kerseymere spotted with black', 'Morning Dress', April 1801

spenceret A fashionable variant of the *spencer.

staylace [stay lace] The lace or cord with which women's *stays and *corsets were threaded, fastened and tightened.

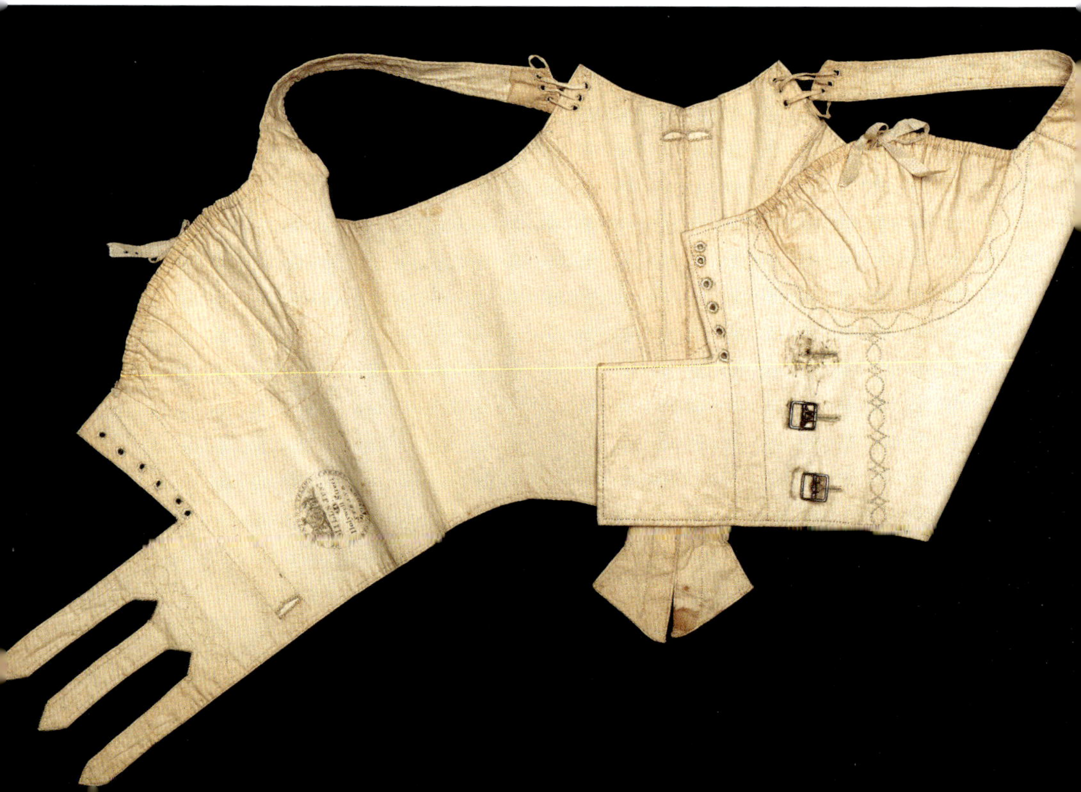

stays (F) A close-fitting undergarment, shaped and stiffened with *whalebone, *cording, canvas or a *busk, or made of leather, closed with lacing, which shaped women's torsos and supported the breasts, with or without shoulder straps. They also added a

layer of warmth and could be padded to enhance the figure. Some stays included knitted 'elastic' fabrics for ease of wear. 'Short stays' reached from the bust to the waist, with shoulder straps, and were a new development in this period. 'Long stays' consisted of a stiffened bodice, reaching the hips, with a centre-front busk and shoulder straps. The term 'stays' started to converge with the term *corset, properly a lighter, softer garment, in the early nineteenth century, until the two became synonymous by about 1820 (in 1803, a staymaker received a patent for 'Long stays, short stays and corsets'). Like corsets, stays created the high, lifted and separated bust style that was the essential foundation of the high-waisted gown styles of this era. *See also* *bosom friend, *Circassian corset, *jumps, *waistcoat.

Pair of cotton twill stays, missing the front busk, c.*1805–15*

stocking purse *See* *purse.

stockings (F) Leg coverings, knee-length or extending above the knee; they were held up by *garters tied under or over the knee for women. They were made of silk, cotton, linen ('*thread'), and wool or *worsted, and in every possible colour. White and pale colours were the most common. Cotton stockings came in stout, fine, superfine and extra superfine qualities, and were originally imitations of silk ones. Stockings could be embellished by embroidery, and by decorative patterns knitted over the instep and at the ankle (*clock).

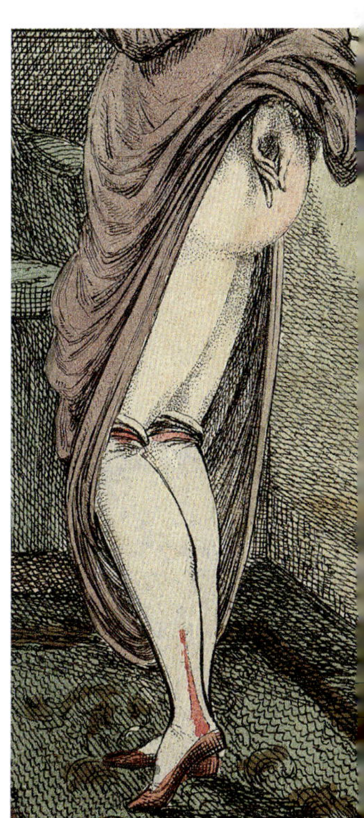

Unknown artist, 'Comfort', c.*1800*

Mills Junr, cotton transitional stays, c.*1795–1800*

stole A long, slender scarf or *tippet, usually of a warm material with a pile, but also of woven fabric. *See also* *boa.

stomacher A panel covering or inserted into the front of a woman's *bodice, or inserted into the front of *jumps or *stays under the lacing. The phrase 'stomacher front' is sometimes used by dress historians to describe the fall-front *gown closures of the late 1790s and 1800s, but it did not have this meaning at the time.

string purse *See* *purse.

tail (F) The *train of a skirt.

tippet A woman's *stole or scarf, long and narrow, or triangular; it was generally worn for warmth and often made of fur or wool, though it could also be light and decorative, or made of feathers or satin interlined with *wadding. A short tippet reached the waist. As the century progressed, a tippet would more usually mean a short *cape, or wider, somewhat structured stole, *pelerine or capelet.

Ann Frankland Lewis, 'Plate 30, England', 1804

toque A brimless style of *hat made with a crown comprising a cylindrical structure with straight sides of various heights, either covered or wrapped with fabric at the lower edge; or a band with a soft, full crown attached, smaller and fitting closer to the head than a *turban.

Evening dress, 'la toque d'Orléans . . . *composed of . . . soft white satin and British net', February 1818*

train The long back hem of a *gown, extending past floor-length, disappearing from *undress (F) by 1807 and from *full dress (F) in the 1810s (except for *court dress [F]). Also called a *tail.

trencher hat [trencher bonnet] A hat or bonnet made with a flat square crown, worn with a corner centred above the face. Trencher is also the correct description for the classic flat-topped academic 'mortarboard' caps still worn today during graduation. Historically, a 'trencher' was a flat piece of wood, often square, used as a plate, from which the name derives.

'Opera & Evening Full Dresses' (detail), 1 August 1806

trowsers (F) *See* *pantaloons (F).

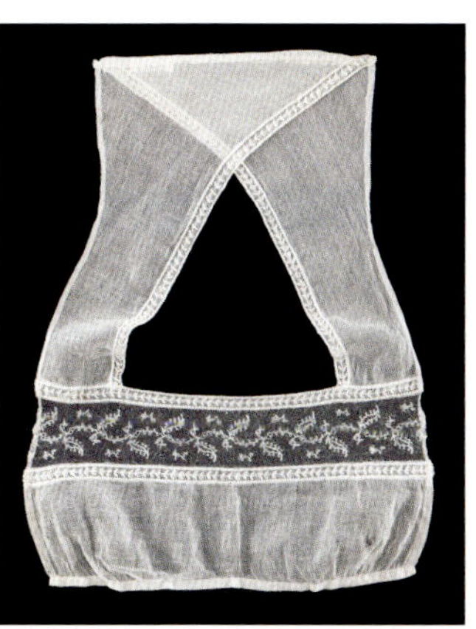

tucker [chemise tucker] A separate edging of linen, *lawn, lace, *muslin or some other fine material, worn around the top of a low-necked bodice and tucked or pinned into it with straight pins, or with a decorative *brooch (J), including at the centre-back neckline.

Indian cotton muslin tucker embroidered with whitework, with an inset of cotton bobbin net, c.1820

tunic [tunic dress] In fashionable use, a knee-length *gown, often sleeveless and loose, worn over an evening gown; *see also* *robe. A tunic dress had the undergown made as part of the ensemble.

Isaac Cruikshank, The Lending Library *(detail), 1800–11*

turban [turban hat, turban cap] A round headdress, inspired by the headwear of various Eastern cultures; it consisted of a length of fabric sewn permanently into shape or simply wound around the head and pinned. Though worn by both men and women, turbans were most common as a form of women's headwear, and were extremely popular for evening wear, especially by older women. The style suited the draped windswept fashions of the late 1790s and continued to evolve through the early nineteenth century. *See also* *Mameluke cap.

Sampson Towgood Roch, Priscilla, Lady Willoughby de Eresby, *1815 copy of an 1810 miniature by George Saunders*

ugly *See* *calash.

umbrella (F) A spoked, foldable protection from rain, distinct from a *parasol which protected from the sun and did not need to be water-resistant. The poles were plainer than parasols, too, made from wood or metals, with covers made of waxed or oiled silk, or cheap cotton, most commonly a deep green, or other dark colour such as brown, blue or red.

undress [dishabille, negligee] (F) Informal or ordinary dress. For women, this included *morning dress, *walking dress, and any other day dress.

John Constable, The Cooper Sisters of Woodhouse Farm, *1802–6, showing domestic day undress*

veil A piece of fabric worn to cover the head, attached to the *cap, *hat or *bonnet, to protect the face and head from heat, cold, dust and wind, or from being observed; made from light, thin fabrics including *muslin, lace, *bobbin net, *gauze, and similar.

visiting dress *See* *walking dress.

wag[g]oner's sleeve A long, full sleeve gathered (*gauged) at the wrist and sometimes about the upper arm, resembling a rural worker's smock.

waistcoat (F) (1) As female underwear, an upper-body garment, worn under or over the *shirt or the *shift for warmth. It was sleeveless and reached to the waist or hips and was often made of *flannel. In this sense, waistcoat could be used as a synonym for *jumps. (2) An outer bodice or bodice front in the style or shape of a sleeveless waistcoat, like the male garment, sometimes part of a *riding-habit ensemble; hence 'waistcoat front'.

walking dress [promenade dress, visiting dress] Ensembles of gowns with shorter hems made *walking length, and an outer garment such as a *cape, *cloak, *mantelet, *mantle, *pelisse, *redingote, *shawl or *spencer, worn outside the home in public; a kind of *half-dress distinguished from domestic day or *morning dress, by better fabrics, darker colours and extra embellishment, and always worn with a *bonnet, *hat or other *headwear.

'Black satin pelisse, lined with rose-coloured sarsnet'. 'Morning Walking Dress', January 1815

walking length For *walking dress, the hem touching the toes but not the ground, from the late 1800s.

walking shoes Practical sturdy shoes made expressly for walking; made of leather or cotton fabrics such as *jean or *nankeen in black or fawn colours, coming higher up the instep than a *pump or *slipper, often with *latchets to tie them together and keep them on the foot, or laced up. The leather soles were also thicker.

wrap [wrapper, wrapping gown] A loose, full robe, open in front, worn in the morning or at home, going over a *morning gown or a *petticoat and *shirt, and made from cotton fabrics or *flannel. Sometimes used as a general term for any full garment that went over another one, like a *pelisse or *dressing gown, and, in a short form, a *canezou.

White cotton wrapping or dressing gown, c.1815–20

wrap front A bodice made with two sides crossing over each other.

Unknown artist, miniature portrait of a woman, 1800–1

wrapping cloak A cloak that covers and wraps around the body from shoulder to hip or below, contrasting with a *scarfed cloak.

wrapping gown *See* *wrap.

York tans (F) Leather *gloves in a buff, bark or tan colour, of a slightly higher quality than ordinary tan leather, popular for riding or driving, worn by men and women, but in different cuts. They are mentioned very frequently in fashion discussions in magazines.

'Pale York tan gloves'. 'Morning Walking Dresses', 1 August 1808

MEN

'I had mounted a new coat from *Davies of Cork Street*, in the true Bond Street cut, with a pair of flesh-coloured silk pantaloons, stockings to match, and a most delicate pair of shoes by Hoby, right and left.'[13]

Memoirs of an Old Wig, 1815

The noticeably shorter poem accompanying the one quoted at the start of the Women chapter (see p. 27) tells the reader 'How to Pack a Gentleman's Portmanteau':

Coat, Waistcoat, and Breeches, shirts, stockings and shoes,
With Handkerchiefs, Nightcap and gown,
A Comb and two Razors, and Tooth-brush compleat,
All you want, when you travel to Town.

For men, the basic ensemble comprised *coat, *waistcoat (pronounced 'wesket') and knee-length *breeches ('britches'), often held up with *braces. They were worn over the *shirt and *stockings. A *nightcap and *nightgown were for sleeping in. The presence of 'two Razors' bespeaks the importance of being clean-shaven with a sharp blade: it appears that this gentleman will have no opportunity to sharpen his razors, so is doubling up. Again, personal care is discussed in the chapter on Hair and Beauty.

One of the reasons this poem is shorter than the female version is that men wore fewer ornamental accessories than women; their fashions changed less rapidly and markedly; and stylistic change came through adjustments of cut and material. In the 1790s men's coats

Sir Thomas Lawrence, Lord Granville Leveson-Gower, later first Earl Granville, *between 1804 and 1809*

had front openings in a tapered 'swallowtail' style and waistcoats with angled 'skirts' covering the groin. Through the 1790s waistcoat skirts rose and were cut straight, across the top of the breeches. By *c.*1800, double- or single-breasted coats were open below the waist with two 'tails' at the back, *cut-in at the waist in a square or inverted U-shaped curve. The large turned-back collar, emphasising the shoulders, could be finished with velvet. *Frock coat styles edged back into fashion around 1815 to see coats regain their skirts, usually made double-breasted. Tightly *fulled (felted after weaving) cloth allowed edges to be cut without the textile fraying, creating a crisp edge around the coat, as well as knife-sharp M- and then V-notched lapels. Sleevehead volume kept pace with women's – tight to the armhole *c.*1800, then slowly expanding to become pleated and full by 1820. New ankle-length tight *pantaloons or loose *trousers added choices to male legwear. The greatest change was in fabrics. A good deal of the decorative possibilities of bright colours, silks and cotton prints withdrew into the space of waistcoats and *neckerchiefs, and plain wool reigned as the outer fabric of choice, complemented by lighter linen and cotton fabrics for summer wear.

Menswear achieved the beginnings of modernity in the Regency, when the popularity of wool in subdued colours for outerwear merged with the idea that a coat should display its quality through excellent fit, improving the wearer's figure – the 'true Bond Street cut' extolled in the opening quote (see p. 93). The principles of men's suits, the subtle skills of tailors, and conventions of formal menswear that still hold today, have their origins in the early nineteenth century. Another point to remember is that, while men's clothing was less varied than women's in styles and fabric, each element of Regency male dress cost roughly double its female equivalent. Men shopped less often but spent more money when they did – a fact that is not highlighted in critiques of fashionability at the time, which are usually centred on supposedly frivolous female consumption.

Over the years people have attributed every single one of the major changes in male dress over the period *c*.1795–1820 directly to trendsetter George 'Beau' Brummell (1788–1840) as an individual, especially the move to darker, less patterned, and more sombre textiles and colours. This was not the case. He did not single-handedly invent the new regimes of masculine dress, but instead he best distilled the changes which had been building for two decades into an influential personal style and the acme of good taste. Around him, the look spread successfully in British society. The revolutions of fit, sobriety and perfection that this society gentleman achieved were all the more radical because he was not a member of the aristocracy. Brummell's influence marked the rise of the gentry class as tastemakers, a new *beau monde*. His force of personality and capacity for style-setting allowed him to dictate to the Prince Regent himself. Brummell epitomised a new standard of elegance and ideal of perfection in male dress.[14] He helped to strengthen the reputation of the English as standard-setters for fashionable male dress by introducing 'a perfection of restrained taste', and 'a nice blend of careless ease and absolute control'.[15]

The elements of sartorial sobriety that Brummell brought to perfection comprised eschewing 'all ornamentation apart from brass buttons on his plain cloth coat, and a heavy gold watch and chain. He shunned patterns and bright colours, limiting himself to plain coats of blue, or perhaps green, with contrasting waistcoat and buff breeches or pantaloons. Evening wear comprised a blue or black coat, white waistcoat, black pantaloons, and pumps. Apart from plain dress with immaculate cut and fit . . . his linen was always whiter than white; his neckcloths starched and uncreased.'[16] These general ideals of sobriety and simplicity in male dress can be seen repeatedly in Regency portraiture as part of the new changes in fashion.

New developments in tailoring relied on the malleable, shapeable qualities of woollen cloths, especially *broadcloth, *hunter, *kersey,

*Melton, *superfine and other *coatings. Because these were heavily milled and fulled, the edges could be cut without fraying (like modern felt), and these edges – left raw, and not turned over – predominate in surviving examples of menswear. Crisp edges were essential to creating the sharp lines of the *collar notch at the lapels. Pantaloons were often made from fabrics with stretch in them – 'elastic' in contemporary parlance. Knitted cotton or silk fabrics of varying quality were employed: thick for day, and finer for evening wear.

Parts of Coats and Legwear, 1817

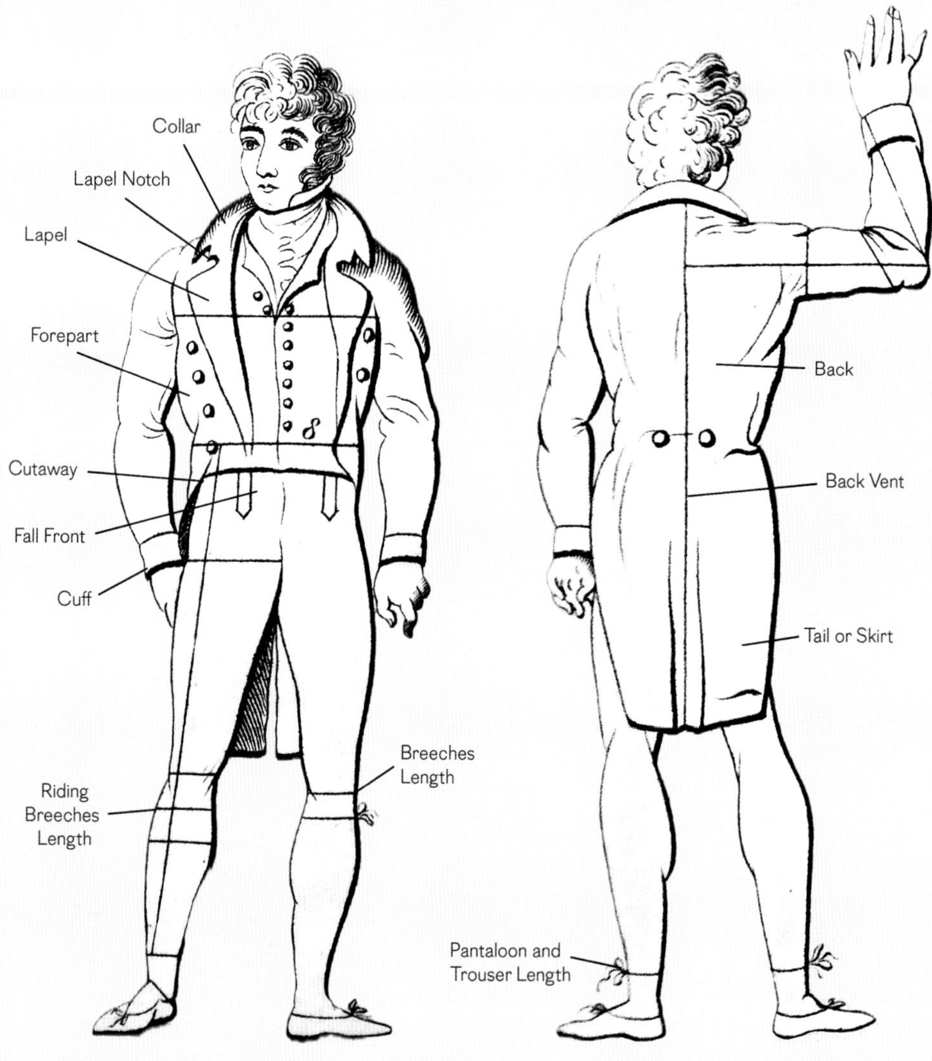

GLOSSARY

Anglesea trousers [Anglesea trowsers] From *c.*1820 onwards, *trousers with a full top pleated into the waistband like *Cossacks, but narrowing to a straight trouser leg.

apron (M) A square, rectangular or shaped garment worn at the front of the body by working men, tying around the waist, to protect the clothes underneath, usually made of sturdy or washable textiles.

article A euphemism for *breeches.

ball dress (M) The ensemble worn at a ball. Men wore *evening dress or *dress, though legwear made from stretch material like black silk jersey could make moving a little easier; as could *breeches which allowed a full bend at the knee. Rules for the Bath assembly rooms decreed no *boots or *half-boots were to be worn in the ballroom (though after 1800 officers on duty were exempt).

Robert Cruikshank, 'Quadrilles. Third Set' (detail), 1817–20

bandanna [bandana, bandano, bandanno, bamdana] A coloured silk or cotton twill or plain woven handkerchief, often red or blue, with white or yellow spots; originally from India, called *bandhani*. The handkerchief was dyed its main colour first, then the pattern was discharged from it with chemicals, leaving the bleached motif behind.

Unknown artist, Portrait of a Sailor (Paul Cuffe?), *c.1800*

banyan [banian, bannian, India gown] A loose, informal man's robe, *nightgown or *dressing-gown, originally from India, made in cotton, silk or wool; it was worn at home, before one was formally dressed.

Barcelona [Barsalona] handkerchief A twilled silk *handkerchief measuring around 20 to 28 inches (50–70 cm) square; plain, checked or with fancy patterns, and usually brightly coloured. Handkerchiefs of this kind were first manufactured in Spain, then in England.

bathing dress (M) Ensembles of clothing worn to bathe at the seaside or in natural springs at spa towns. At spas, men wore long-sleeved *waistcoats and *drawers of brownish linen, or long, smock-like garments. In the sea, men could also wear *shirts and linen drawers, or nothing at all.

bearer A band behind the *fall on *breeches, *trousers and *pantaloons, reaching across from each side and buttoned down the midline; it was narrower in the middle than at the sides, and rose an inch or two above the top of the fall.

Belcher handkerchief A patterned *handkerchief, usually yellow and red, sometimes blue with white spots, named after the prize-fighter Jem Belcher (1781–1811), boxing champion of All England, 1800–5.

Charles Allingham, Jem Belcher, *c.1800–1*

bicorne Man's *hat with brim turned up to make a front and a back flap. Often decorated with a fringed edge, and *rosette or other emblem on the side. Frequently worn in uniform contexts.

Bluchers [Blucher boots, Blucher army boots] *Half-boots, loose around the ankle, similar to *Wellington boots but using less leather and easier to put on.

boots (M) Calf- to knee-high footwear – originally worn only for horseback riding, in the country, or on carriages – which became generally popular during the 1790s, helped by a new democratisation of fashion, the martial allure of the boot-wearing army during the ongoing wars with the French, and the development of close-fitting *pantaloons that could be worn inside boots. Boots cost twice as much as *shoes, both to buy and to maintain. They were kept on boot trees to retain their shape. They were closer fitting in the 1790s and early 1800s, then became somewhat loose. Boots were distinguished between those having a back strap, such as *top or jockey boots, and *Hessians and *Wellington boots which were 'elastic', that is, often created with crimps or pleats over the instep to allow for better movement. *See also* *Bluchers, *half-boots, *Hussar boots.

James Gillray, 'A pair of polished gentlemen', 1801, depicting a Hessian boot (left) and top boot (right)

box coat [riding coat, driving coat] A kind of *great coat: a heavy, loose, knee- to ankle-length overcoat with one or more *capes, worn by coachmen and any travellers seated outside a coach. The name comes from the 'box' a coachman sat upon to drive.

The back was cut more loosely than a *surtout, with a single vent at the centre-back *skirt. It had to be cut particularly loose as it could be worn over two to three under-coats, including a great coat.

braces A pair of straps, either two individual ones crossing (braces) or two joined into a single strap at the back (suspenders), made of leather, canvas, silk and other materials, passing over the shoulders and fastening to *buttons on *breeches, *trouser or *pantaloon waistbands, one on each side in front, and one either side of the back vent, to hold the legwear up and keep the line of the legwear taut. They were popular from the 1790s and allowed the waistband to be made less tight, as it no longer did all the work of suspending legwear. Also called breeches slings, gallows, gallowses, gallaces.

'The Protean Figure and Metamorphic Costumes' paper doll, 1811

breeches Men's legwear reaching to, and fastened, just below the knee, with a *fall front or flap opening, multiple pockets, and an adjustable lacing panel at the centre back; they were always worn with *stockings,

which covered the lower leg. With the advent of *braces, *c.*1790, a slimmer silhouette replaced the earlier fuller cut. Breeches were distinct from *trousers, which covered the whole leg; from *c.*1800 trousers began to supersede breeches, which were consigned to wear by the elderly and to *evening dress and formal *court dress. Fabrics for daywear included *buckskin, *buff, *corduroy, *fustian, *jean, *kerseymere, *leather, *nankeen and *velverets. For evening wear, kerseymere, nankeen and knitted silk. Euphemisms included articles, galligaskins, ineffables, inexplicables, inexpressibles, kicks, kickeys, *small clothes, rum kicks (made of brocade, or embellished with gold or silver) and *unmentionables. Pronounced 'britches'.

Robert Dighton, Molineaux *[boxer Tom Molineaux], 1812*

buckskins Breeches made from *buckskin (T), often worn for riding.

buskins *See* *Hussar boots.

cane A kind of walking stick, with a straight top and no curve or crook, often with a string or lace at the top for hanging it from the wrist, or a decorative tassel.

cape (M) The attached circular addition(s) falling from under the collar of a *cloak or *great coat and draping over the shoulders to provide extra warmth. Men's clothing could have anywhere from one to five capes attached, especially for *riding or *box coats.

chapeau-bras *See* *opera hat.

chitterlings Slang for *shirt frills.

cloak (M) A loose outer garment, worn over other clothing for warmth and protection outside. It was like a *cape, gathered or cut in a semi-circle, fastening around the neck and falling to the knees or lower – three-quarter or full length – and usually had a second elbow-length cape layer around the upper body. Cloaks were lighter than *coats and easy to put on and take off without disturbing the clothing underneath, or trying to put a coat sleeve into another sleeve. 'Hard' cloaks were made of *worsted fabric.

coat The basic upper outer garment for men, generally made from wool in dark colours such as black, blue, dark brown or green, or for summer or sporting wear, in lighter linen and cotton fabrics of white to paler brown. Sometimes called a common, body or close-bodied coat, distinguishing it by the proximity to the body from a *great coat that could be worn over it. The fashionability and quality of a coat lay in its fabric, construction, and surface texture (for wools). Tailors manipulated wool cloth to stretch, shrink and accommodate shaping, adding careful interior padding and tactical darts to create coats that, at their best, enhanced the male form into a better version of its natural self. Gilt *buttons were preferred for evening coats, self-covered or silk-

Jean-Auguste-Dominique Ingres,
Portrait of Lord Grantham *(detail), 1816*

thread buttons for garments to be worn at other times. The cut of day-coats sat close, but easy to the shoulders instead of tight, the skirts hanging smoothly. Images of coats in wear show that they were buttoned quite tightly across the torso. The coat that fitted the wearer like a second skin should have been unnoticeable, when compared to an ill-fitting one. The fashionable cut moved from a 'swallowtail' line with an upright *collar and no lapels in 1795 to the cutaway *tail coat, with a folded-down collar and lapels by around 1800. Coats could be single- or double-breasted, with a variety of collar styles. Sleeves were long, narrow and cut to the natural bend of the arm, ending over the hand with a side slit at the cuff closed by two or three buttons, or with a small, rounded cuff. *See* *box coat, *dress coat, *driving coat, *evening coat, *frock coat, *great coat, *hunting coat, *morning coat, *Petersham coat, *riding coat, *surtout, *top coat.

cocked hat *See* *opera hat.

collar (M) A *coat's collar was an important part of its style. It could be of *velvet, to contrast with a wool coat, and have different constructions and therefore shapes, such as the stand, roll or Prussian collar. Where the collar met the lapel, a V- or M-shape could be created, the latter not used before 1800 but popular by 1803. An 1807 fashion plate called this 'cut into a heart'.[17]

Man's wool coat (collar detail), 1810–20

cork bottom shoes *Boots or *shoes with an extra cork sole between the outer and inner leather soles, for insulation against cold, like *clogs.

Cossacks Voluminous *trousers introduced in 1814, when Tsar Alexander I attended the celebrations in London of the Peace of Vienna, accompanied by Cossack soldiers wearing a similar style. They were pleated into a waistband and drawn in at the ankles with a *ribbon drawstring, and could have a centre-front button fly instead of a *fall front.

Robert Cruikshank, 'Quadrilles. Third Set' (detail), 1817–20

court dress (M) The highest, most formal version of *full dress fulfilling the regulations for appearing at court. Men's court dress was a full dress *coat, without collar or lapels, made of silk, velvet or woollen cloth, and often richly embroidered in gold, silver or coloured silk, worn with matching *breeches and *waistcoat, white silk *stockings, and *pumps with *buckles. Any full dress naval or military uniform was considered appropriate.

Unknown artist, 'A Gentleman in a Court Dress', 1809

cravat A long and narrow, or square folded into a triangle, piece of light linen, cotton or silk fabric, wrapped around the neck and tied in a knot or bow at the front, in black and coloured silk, in addition to the usual white colour. *See also* *neckcloth.

cut-in The transitional curve or corner between the front of a *coat with no *skirt, and the *tail (M) at the back.

dickey A man's false, detachable shirt front.

dishabille *See* *undress.

ditto suit [dittoes, suit of dittoes] A man's suit with *breeches, *waistcoat and *coat made from the same fabric. The term was often used for black professional or brown sporting dress. 'Dittoes' was also used to describe a group of men all dressed in a similar manner.

Sir Henry Raeburn, Reverend Robert Walker (1755–1808) Skating on Duddingston Loch *('The Skating Minister'), 1795*

drawers (M) Knee-length linen, cotton, fine knit or woollen underwear trousers, knee-length and worn under *breeches, acting as removable washable linings, especially for leather breeches. Drawers were joined at the crotch except at the front, on a broad waistband, with the same diagonal cut as breeches, and with similar extra fabric and room to move over the buttocks, and tied about the knee with tapes or 'strings' at the cuff. Euphemisms included smalls, *small clothes and *unmentionables.

Cream wool flannel drawers, 1800–20

dress (M) (1) The ensemble of clothing worn. (2) *Full or *evening dress, a contrast and complement to *undress. The distinctions between 'dress' and 'undress' were often small, and indicated by differences in the materials, colours, and nature of the *buttons or accessories.

dress coat A coat worn for *dress (M2) at dinner, the opera, and other late afternoon to evening events. Frequently dark blue, could also be dark green, brown or burgundy. Black became more general towards the end of the 1810s and was required for *full dress. Dress coats were cut tight across the waist and chest; they could have round cuffs, with no slits. *Cf.* *morning coat.

dressing-gown (M) A loose wrap reaching to the ground, tied round the waistband without a back-vent, with more fitted structure around the neck and shoulders, and set-in sleeves, into the 1810s, made from cotton, linen, *flannel or silk, sometimes padded or quilted. Similar to a *morning gown. *Cf.* *banyan, *nightgown.

driving coat *See* *box coat.

ears A name for the points of the *shirt *collar when they were starched and high enough to reach and rest on the jawline, especially in the 1810s.

evening coat A *dress coat.

evening dress (M) A form of *dress, comprising clothing and accessories suitable only for evening events. Men required a dark coat, white or black *neckcloth, white *waistcoat, and white, tan or black *pantaloons or *breeches (correct for evening dress until *c.*1810) closed by silk strings or buckles. (*Cf.* *morning dress.) Footwear was *pumps or low-fronted shoes.

fall [falls, fall-down, fall-front] Referring to the fall-front opening of *breeches or, later, *pantaloons and *trousers, comprising a flap of material sewn along its lower edge and

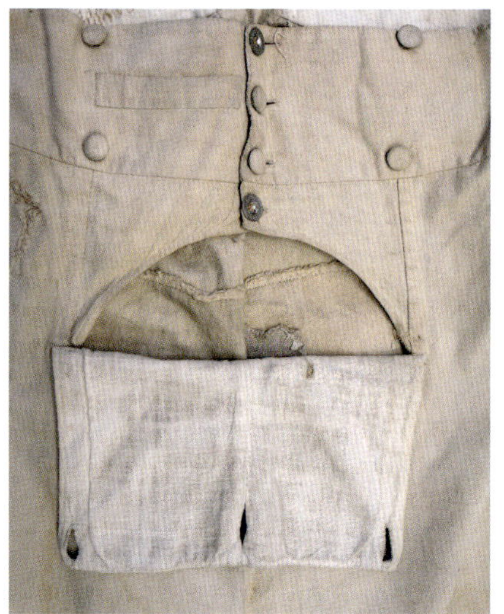

buttoned to (or just below) the waistband. 'Whole' falls extended from one side-seam to the other, while the more fashionable 'small' or 'split' falls consisted of a smaller central flap. Falls attached to the *bearer.

Cotton trousers, c.*1820, with small fall and bearer*

false calves *Stockings made from *fleecy-hosiery over the calves to pad out the area and give a shapely effect; or separate shaped cork or wool pads to wear inside the stockings.

fob [fob pocket] A small pocket in the waistband of the *breeches, used for carrying a watch, money, or other valuables. *See also* *fob (J).

frock coat A double- or single-breasted *coat, with lapels and full thigh- to knee-length *skirts, with no cut-away to make tails, appearing in the mid-1810s based on a military style.

William Owen,
Sir Thomas Dyke Acland, *1808*

full dress [*dress] (M) An ensemble or a mode of dress appropriate for formal or public occasions in the afternoon or later, such as *court dress, *evening dress, or dress worn to the opera or formal dinners. (*Cf.* *half-dress.) It required silk *stockings, and a white or black *waistcoat.

'Full Dress of a Gentleman', April 1810

gaiter pantaloons *See* *moscheetos.

gaiters [spatterdashes, knee-caps] (M) Leg coverings made of leather, canvas, *fustian, *drill, *kerseymere or wool, extending from above the knee or from the calf to the front of the foot, and fastened with buttons down the outer side. Worn with *breeches by working men, or by middle- and upper-class men in the countryside, gaiters protected the legs and legwear, and kept stones out of shoes. Half-gaiters, short gaiters or *spats extended from the ankle to the front of the foot and were worn with *trousers and *pantaloons.

Pair of brown linen gaiters, 1800–17

gallows [gallowses, gallaces] *See* *braces.

gloves (M) A covering for the whole of the hand, usually with individual fingers. Made from light, thin, flexible materials, especially leathers such as *beaver (4), *buff, doeskin, *chamois, *kid, *lambskin and *wash-leather; and textiles including knitted or woven cotton, silk, *jean, *nankeen, *worsted, wool, *vicuna and linen. Glove leathers were cured with alum instead of tanning, which made them softer and more pliable, and consumers distinguished between gloves that could be washed and those that could not. The only acceptable colours for *full dress gloves were white or a buff tan. French gloves were considered the best, but were restricted from import to Britain. Gloves could be lined with *fleecy-hosiery or *fur for winter. *See also* *York tans.

great coat A general term for any form of outer coat going over a man's common *coat, intended to protect the wearer and his clothes out of doors, especially when travelling and during wet weather. In cold but dry weather, a *spencer was preferable. Made of heavy material, and heavy to wear, it was usually single-breasted (though could be double-breasted) and covered the wearer to the knee, calf or ankle; it was fastened in front with straps, in addition to, or instead of, buttons, and often had a *cape or capes over the shoulders. *See also* *box coat, *driving coat, *surtout.

half-boot (M) Footwear shorter than the full knee-high *boots, reaching to the middle of the calf. Laced half-boots fastened up the centre front from the top of the vamp and were just over ankle height. *See also* *highlows.

half-gaiter *See* *gaiter.

James Pollard, Cottager's Hospitality to Travellers of The Coach Broke Down *(detail), showing men wearing a variety of greatcoats, 1819*

handkerchief (M) A generic word for a square of finished fabric, plain or decorated, worn around the head, neck or shoulders, usually of cotton or linen, or silk when used as a *neckerchief around the neck. For men, coloured handkerchiefs were only acceptable as *morning dress or *undress. In *evening dress, white or black only was allowed, the origin of modern black or white tie conventions. A smaller, carried handkerchief of cotton or linen was called a 'pocket handkerchief'. *See also* *belcher, *neckerchief.

Hugh Douglas Hamilton, Lord Edward Fitzgerald, c.*1796–8*

hat (M) Structured headwear made with a crown and brim, of wool, fur or silk in dark or middling colours such as fawn or drab; also straw, *chip and *Leghorn. Castor or *beaver hats were made of hair, wool, and some beaver fur. Plated hats were silk *floss covered with beaver. Historically, the best hats were made wholly of beaver fur imported from North America. Declining beaver populations, import costs, and war with America and French-controlled Canada contributed to the rise in woollen imitations. Silk hats could be lined with cane to give them the stiffness that felted hats had naturally. The high-crowned hat with a flat top and narrow turned-up brim was fashionable from about 1797, becoming the ubiquitous top hat of the later nineteenth century. These tall hats could have vertical sides and flat crowns, or sides that narrowed slightly upwards, or else widened towards the top. Low hats had shallower crowns and wider brims. *See also* *bicorne, *opera hat, *top hat, *tricorne.

Black beaver hat with a black silk brim underside, silk hatband fastened with a small buckle, c.*1820*

Hessians Men's black, square-toed *riding boots, of a style first worn by the troops of Hesse, Germany, and popular from the mid-1790s; they were upper-calf-length at the back, and, in front, curved to a point just below the knee, with a decorative tassel in the centre. They also had a slightly curved back seam. Hessians sometimes had a narrow border of coloured leather bound around the upper edge.

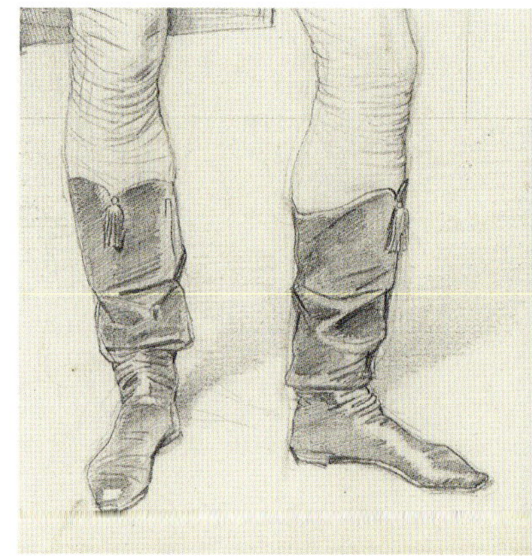

Jean-Auguste-Dominique Ingres, Portrait of Lord Grantham *(detail), 1816*

highlows [high-lows] A kind of *half-boot or ankle boot, or shoes that reached to the ankle, tying with leather thongs, considered informal, functional or country wear, not fashionable.

hunting coat A single-breasted woollen coat buttoning to the collarbone, with little to no lapel, a turnback *collar, foreparts extending into a *skirt at the front with no waist seam (unlike a *frock coat), often with three buttons down each side of the back vent, and one on the lower back-vent hem corner. Worn for hunting, riding and outdoor sport.

James Ward, Theophilus Levett and a Favourite Hunter *(detail), 1817*

Hussar boots *Boots resembling *Hessians but without the centre-front tassel. Also called buskins.

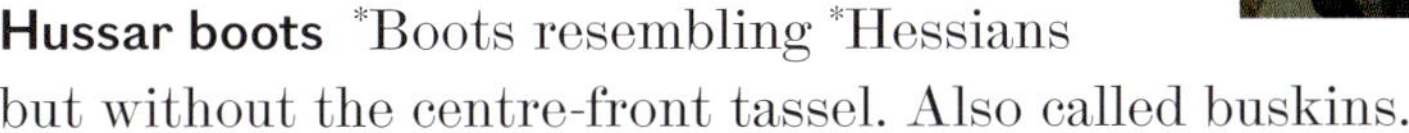

India gown *See* *banyan.

inexpressibles A euphemism for *breeches.

jacket (M) Any short, close-fitting outer *coat. For men, it was often indistinguishable from a sleeved *waistcoat.

jockey waistcoat A *waistcoat with vertical instead of horizontal stripes.

kicks A euphemism for *breeches.

latchets The pair of long tabs at the top front of a *shoe that overlap and pass through the *buckle to fasten closed, or tie together with a lace without overlapping.

lining *Coats were either partially or fully unlined and, where they were lined, it was often only where the inside would show. Lining fabrics were made of linen, *fustian, *worsted, twilled silk (especially silk *serge (2)), or combinations of these fabrics, often in the same garment, depending on where they were placed. Sleeves were always lined, to help the arm slide through them, usually with a plainer fabric such as a glazed cotton or linen. Silk could appear only as a thin band at the cuffs. Coat *tails were unlined. *Breeches, *pantaloons and *trousers were unlined except at the tops, waistbands, pockets and *falls, usually in a cotton or linen fabric, with silk *serge (2) used in more formal or *dress apparel or just on the falls. *Great coats which went over coats were more usually lined through the body to reduce friction between the two layers. *Waistcoats were usually wholly lined in plain fabrics not meant to be seen.

list shoes [list slippers] Soft, thick, warm footwear for both sexes made from *list, the selvedges of woollen textiles cut off by weavers and clothworkers and re-woven into a new textile, lined with *baize. List footwear was worn as *undress indoors, in carriages, by the sick, and by those who cared for them, as the soft soles made no noise.

low hat *See* *hat.

military folding hat *See* *opera hat.

morning coat A less formal *coat for *morning dress, with plated *buttons, made of *kerseymere or *superfine, and lighter linen or cotton cloths in summer, especially *nankeen. Could have slit cuffs with buttons. *Cf.* *dress coat.

morning dress (M) An ensemble or a mode of dress for informal daywear at home or outdoors in the hours before the afternoon. For men, indoor morning dress could be a loose robe such as a *nightgown; for outdoor wear they might wear a

'MORNING DRESSES for Sept: 1807'

light-coloured or lightweight *coat with plated, rather than gilt, buttons, and correspondingly light-coloured, lightweight legwear and a plain *waistcoat. (*Cf.* *evening dress.) Could be called negligee.

morning gown (M) One of many names for a long, loose, open robe worn in the morning and in private, variously called *dressing-gown', *banyan, or the old-fashioned *nightgown or *powdering-gown. Colder-weather gowns could be lined with flannel or fur for warmth.

Andrew Geddes, Sir David Wilkie, *wearing a morning gown, 1816*

moscheetos [gaiter pantaloons, moschettos, moskeetos, musquetos, musquettos] *Pantaloon-like trousers with an extension over the front of the foot, like *gaiters, supposedly intended originally to give protection against mosquitoes.

Pair of buff cotton moscheetos, worn by Frederick Bowman, c.1815

mourning dress (M) Black and sombre-coloured clothing and accessories worn as a public display of grief and mourning for a death in the family, or in the extended royal family. The closeness of the relationship determined the length and degree of mourning dress. Male mourning dress was less prescriptive than women's. Full mourning required all black clothes, with 'weepers' – a strip of white linen or *muslin worn on the coat cuff. Lesser mourning could be conveyed by a black arm band, as well as black gloves.

neckcloth Any fabric item worn around the neck; commonly a square or rectangle made of white linen or cotton fabrics, it was worn over the collar and tied to hold it closed. Patterned and coloured neckcloths were informal choices for daywear. *See also* *bandanna, *cravat, *handkerchief, *neckerchief, stock.

John Smart, Portrait of Lieutenant Colonel John Wingfield, *1803*

neckerchief [neck-handkerchief] (M) A square, finished piece of cloth, worn around the neck, especially by working men. Neckerchiefs were made in a huge variety of printed or woven coloured cottons and silks. *See also* *bandanna, *cravat, *handkerchief.

negligee [negligé, negligée] *See* *undress, *morning dress.

nightcap (M) Any soft, unstructured, informal cap worn by men at home or in bed, often knitted, or made of other linen or wool fabrics, part of *undress.[18]

Clockwise from top: two nightcaps, brown angora gloves, cream wool wristlets, three cream wool knee warmers, all knitted, 1800–20

nightgown (M) (1) A loose gown worn to sleep in, made like a *shirt but knee-length. (2) An informal robe, such as a *banyan, *dressing-gown or *powdering-gown, worn at home, especially by men.

nightshirt A knee-length shirt for sleeping, usually made from linen.

Linen nightshirt, 1800–20

opera dress A kind of *evening or *full dress.

opera hat [chapeau-bras, cocked hat, military folding hat] A crescent-shaped, black *hat usually worn for *evening or *full dress, folded up between two brims to allow it to be carried under the arm; it was often trimmed with tassels and feathers.

Charles Williams, 'A bit of flattery', c.1807

pantaloons [tights] (M) A type of close-fitting, calf- or ankle-length men's *trousers, often strapped under the foot, or with a vent on the outer side of each leg. They were not worn as *court or *full dress, but were acceptable as *evening dress, and came into general wear from military use. Pantaloons were often made of knitted material to give them a semi-elastic fit, in thick cotton, wool, or lighter silk; colours were usually pale creams and tans, or black. *See also* *moscheetos.

Pantaloons made of machine-knitted cotton and decorated with silk braid, 1810–20

pantaloon-trousers A combination of *pantaloons and *trousers, tight to the calf then the same width down to the ankles.

pelisse [pelisse-greatcoat] (M) In the male context, originally a term for a *cloak, and in this sense, especially in a military context, a man's cloak, trimmed or lined with fur. British Light Dragoon regiments had started adopting Hussar elements in the 1790s. Four converted fully by 1807 and theirs was the original pelisse – worn over one shoulder like a *cape, fastened with a cord, and festooned with gilt braids and buttons.

'British Off[ice]r of Hussars of the 18th Reg[imen]t in Review Order', from The Military Costume of Europe, *1812*

Petersham coat A style of brown *coat popularised by Charles Stanhope (1780–1851), until 1829 Viscount Petersham.

Petersham Cossacks [Petersham breeches, Petershams] A type of *Cossack trouser popularised by Charles Stanhope, until 1829 Viscount Petersham; excessively loose and spread out over the foot without a drawstring, unlike Cossacks, or drawn in to create a flounce below the string.

Charles Williams, Too long and too loose!! Or Lord Sham-Peter the amateur tailor, *satirising Petersham Cossacks, 1816*

petticoat breeches Men's knee-length trousers, gathered at the waist and correspondingly loose about the legs, with no fastenings at the knees, and thus resembling a *petticoat; they were worn for working, often over other legwear, typically by seafarers.

pocket (M) In men's coats, the pockets were either flapped at the front or hidden in the back pleat, from the mid-1800s. In *breeches, *pantaloons and *trousers, pockets of various sizes were concealed at the waistband and side seams, including the small *fob pocket. The pocket bags were usually made of a stout, plain-weave fabric made from linen, cotton or *fustian.

pocket handkerchief *See* *handkerchief.

powdering-gown A man's informal robe, such as a *banyan, *dressing-gown or *nightgown, originally worn in the morning while the hair was being powdered.

pumps (M) Flat, fine, light, close-fitting dancing or evening *dress *shoes, open over the instep, which were sewn in a turnshoe construction with the upper attached directly to the outer sole, unlike a shoe's construction using a welted rand (strip of leather between the sole and the upper); of fine black *kid or shiny patent leather. Men would often carry their pumps to a ball or evening event and change into the more delicate footwear there.

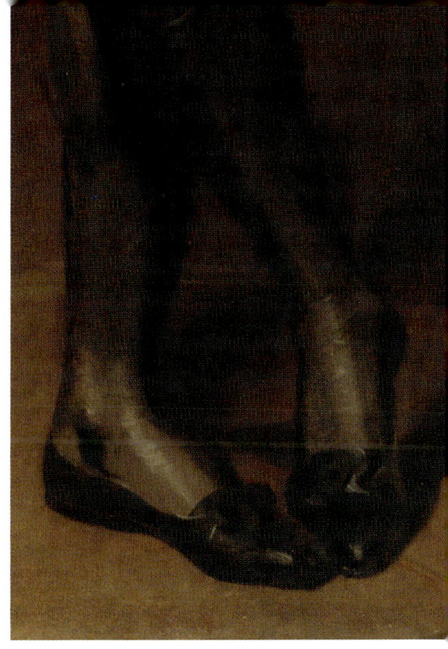

Sir Thomas Lawrence, Lord Granville Leveson-Gower, later first Earl Granville *(detail), between 1804 and 1809*

riding boots *Boots with *spurs.

riding coat A *great coat with at least one *cape, also called a *box coat or *surtout. It combined the weather-protective qualities of a *cloak with sleeves that left the arms free.

riding dress An ensemble worn for riding and driving, or clothing in the same style, which became popular from the late 1790s onwards, as elements of riding clothing traditionally worn on country estates or in the mounted cavalry became normal metropolitan fashion. Examples are wearing *boots instead of *shoes; deep split coat *tails designed for sitting on a horse; *capes and *great coats; *pantaloons for tucking inside boots; and leather *breeches cut with more ease in the seat and knee to accommodate a long day in the saddle. *See also* *box coat, *buckskins, *hunting coat, *riding boots, *riding coat.

Sir Henry Raeburn, George Harley Drummond, *c.1808–9*

shirt (M) The undergarment worn on the upper body next to the skin to protect outer clothing, made of squares and rectangles of white linen of various qualities, and often with a *shirt frill down the front. The *collar and sleeves were prominent, as these parts were visible in the openings of other clothing. The long sleeves ended in single or double (folded-back) cuffs, and could be finely pleated through ironing to get their bulk neatly and easily into tight *coat sleeves. Shirts opened about a foot (30 cm) down the front and fastened at the neck and cuffs, and sometimes in one place at the centre-front opening, with thread or fabric-covered buttons. They reached mid-thigh. If *drawers were not worn, the shirt's tails could be tucked between the legs. The *collar was always square at the edges, but in the later 1810s might have a concave curve cut into the back to create a better fit. Collars closed around the neck with *neckcloths.

White linen shirt, inked with '1812 J.C. 7', 1812

shirt frill A frill of *muslin, *cambric, or other fine linen or cotton fabric contrasting with the denser main fabric of the shirt, gathered down the front opening, and covering any gaps from the slit; frills showed through the waistcoat. 'Chitterlings' was a slang word for the frills.

Linen cambric muslin shirt frill on a linen shirt, c.1810–20

shoes (M) The main kind of footwear, along with *boots, finishing below the ankle and over the instep. Shoes were constructed with the upper lasted to the insole, and a welted rand, in contrast to lighter, finer *pumps. *Undress shoes for daywear had 'short quarters' (the two back sections) and a longer vamp, and *dress shoes had 'long quarters' and a short vamp revealing more of the upper foot. Shoelaces were called 'strings'. Right and left or 'crooked' lasts were beginning to be used more in men's shoes over the older 'straight' lasts with no differentiation. Straights were more comfortable for men with flat feet, or those suffering from gout, rheumatism or corns.

Charles Willson Peale, Portrait of Raphaelle Peale and Titian Ramsay Peale I *(detail), 1795*

skirt The lower part of a coat below the waist.

sleeve buttons Made in pairs, like cufflinks, to join together the cuffs of sleeves through buttonholes.

slip (M) *See* *under waistcoat.

slippers (M) Backless shoes worn at home and informally, often made from red *morocco leather.

Louis-Léopold Boilly, Portrait of Monsieur G. Giving his Daughter a Geography Lesson *(detail), 1812*

small clothes [smalls, small cloths] A euphemism for *drawers or *breeches.

socks Short leg coverings made from knitted linen, silk, *worsted, wool or cotton. They only became common when men's legwear reached the ankle. Also called half-stockings, or pantaloon stockings.

spats [spatts] A military word for a *half-gaiter.

spencer (M) A short-waisted jacket or short *great coat worn over a *coat, with no tails. Originally a masculine garment, the *spencer (F) was soon adopted by women, and in this form is much better known. Fashion histories often attribute the short half-coat's invention to George Spencer, 4th Duke of Marlborough (1739–1817); however, the earliest references in periodicals of around 1795 name the originator as his brother Charles (1740–1820), who 'betted some friends, that he could sport a fashion, the most useless and ridiculous that could be conceived, and that it should . . . be universally adopted'.[19] Other, later versions of the story say a Spencer nobleman either burned off his coat tails in front of the fire or tore one off when riding, and decided to make the truncated jacket a fashion as a way of carrying off the damaged garment. Spencers kept the wearer warm in dry, cold weather but with less weight than a full great coat, though the latter was better for keeping rain off. They were also useful for riding, not having a great coat's long skirts.

Louis-Léopold Boilly, The Public in the Salon of the Louvre, Viewing the Painting of the 'Sacre' *(detail), begun 1808*

spurs A pair of sharp pointed metal objects, usually including a spiked wheel, which buckled onto the heels of *boots, used for urging a horse forward. Spurs were part of military uniform and *riding dress, and often attracted ridicule when worn as fashion in everyday life.

starcher Slang for *neckcloth.

stays (M) Male stays reached from ribs to hips, and reduced and smoothed the waistline and were often worn by dandies. Stays could also support the abdomen and kidneys during exercise and sport.

stick A *cane.

stiffener A starched linen support for a high *cravat or *neckcloth.

stock A man's cotton, linen or silk neckwear. It commonly consisted of a yard (91 cm) width of linen or cotton fabric gathered into tapes or a buckled closure that fastened at the back. A structured version, inspired by military dress, consisted of black or white silk, covering a stiff canvas base, often with a whalebone or metal support inside, and buckling at the back. George IV particularly popularised stocks after 1822, as they held in his abundant neck.

Linen stock, worn by Thomas Coutts, 1800–20

stockings (M) Leg coverings made from knitted linen, silk, *worsted, wool or cotton. Knee-length or extending above the knee; they were held up in menswear often by the knee fastening of the *breeches that were worn over them, or the drawstring of the *drawers. Men could wear two pairs together for warmth, for a fine appearance, or to prevent leg hairs from sticking through fine silk stockings.

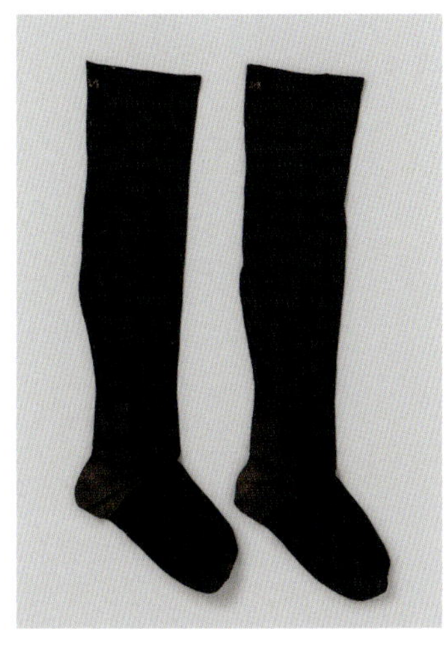

Black cotton and wool stockings, 1800–20

straight waistcoat A *waistcoat with or without a collar, but without a lapel.

suit Men's full ensemble comprising matching coat, waistcoat and legwear: *breeches, *trousers or *pantaloons. During the Regency, the three components of the suit were generally of different colours and materials. If they all matched or were 'ensuite', they could be called a *ditto suit because the colour repeated.

surtout A man's outer *coat, with a *skirt reaching to or below the knees, shorter and closer-fitting than a *great coat and looser-fitting than a *frock coat, with a double-vented back and side pleat pockets with scalloped pocket flap. Often used as a synonym for great coat.

suspenders *See* *braces.

tail (M) The long, narrow back *skirt of a *coat with a cutaway front, in pairs separated by a centre-back vent.

top boots *Boots reaching just below the knee, with turned-over tops in a lighter shade of leather, often brown or tan, and straps on the side for pulling them on. Also called jockey boots.

top coat A man's coat intended to protect the wearer and his clothes out of doors. Of lighter cloth than a *great coat and suitable for walking.

Thomas Uwins, John Thomas Bigge, *1819*

top hat Any wool or silk *hat with a tall straight crown and narrow brim.

tricorne Hat with brim turned up in three places to form a triangular shape, usually made of felt. Common throughout the eighteenth century, but considered old-fashioned or working dress by the Regency period. Could be decorated with a fringed edge, braid or feathers.

trousers [trowsers, trowzers] (M) Long, loose legwear with a *fall front, reaching below the knee or to the ankle, contrasting with knee-length and close-fitting *breeches, or long and tight *pantaloons. Trousers had existed for a long time as working dress. During the 1790s, this piece of informal clothing became increasingly widespread as fashion, acceptable for *half-dress by about 1808 and as *evening dress by 1817. For daywear, made from utilitarian, often pale-coloured textiles such as cotton, *duck, *jean, linen, *nankeen and *moleskin. Lighter pairs for hot weather could be called 'summer trousers'. *See also* *Anglesea trousers, *Cossacks, *Petersham Cossacks.

Beige cotton trousers with bone and covered buttons, 1800–20

umbrella (M) A spoked, foldable protection from rain, with plain poles made from wood or metals, with covers made of waxed or oiled silk, or cheap cotton, usually a deep green, or other subdued colour, especially brown, blue or red. They were first introduced in the 1750s.

under waistcoat [slip] An upper-body sleeveless garment cut like a normal *waistcoat (M1) but worn under that garment as a warm lining, with the body made of *flannel or other utilitarian material, and only a tailored *collar and small facing in an appropriate waistcoat textile appearing at the chest below the main waistcoat.

Flannel under waistcoat with a broadcloth visible collar, 1800–20

undress [dishabille, negligee] (M) Informal, looser or ordinary day dress. For men, it applied to *morning dress worn at home, clothing worn informally out of doors, and sporting clothing.

Two kinds of undress, 'The Art of Ingeniously Tormenting', 1808: 1. Morning undress for home; 2. Morning or walking undress for public

unmentionables A euphemism for *drawers or *breeches.

vamp The front upper part of the *shoe.

vest An outer *waistcoat.

waistcoat (M) (1) Unless otherwise specified, a short, sleeveless upper-body garment, worn as outerwear by men under a *coat or *jacket, sometimes two at a time. Waistcoat backs were made of a plainer cotton, linen, silk or *worsted, and adjusted at the lower back with *buckles on a strip, or pairs of tapes. Working men wore sleeved waistcoats reaching to the waist, which differ from jackets as being cut close to fit under a coat. These could have the sleeves made of the main fabric, or in a plain lining fabric, not meant to be seen. (2) As underwear, an upper-body garment buttoning down the front, worn under or over the shirt for warmth, often made of *flannel or *wash-leather, with elbow- or full-length sleeves, opening all the way down the front, fastened with buttons, and reaching to the hips. *See also* *straight waistcoat, *under waistcoat.

A straight waistcoat of green silk, 1810s

walking dress A term for *morning dress worn in public.

Wellington boots Originally, high *boots rising to the knee and cut away behind, like *Hessians. The term was later also applied to slightly shorter boots worn under *trousers, or any formal but still relatively high boots. They were named for Arthur Wellesley, 1st Duke of Wellington (1769–1852), and popularised by him. Similar to a *top boot but without the turnover top, which made them easier to wear under trousers.

Wellington boot, from The Whole Art of Dress!, *1830*

Wellington pantaloons *Pantaloons with side slits from the calf down, fastened by loops and buttons.

wristlets Knitted separate woollen cuffs for keeping the wrists warm in cold weather. *See* image for *nightcap (p. 117).

York tans (M) Leather *gloves in a buff, bark or tan colour, of a slightly higher quality than ordinary tan leather, popular for riding or driving, worn by men and women, but in different cuts.

HAIR
&
BEAUTY

not loaded
Eau de
de Rose

'With the stiffness of cloth of gold and embroidered tissues, have also disappeared the enormous pile of hair, furbelows, feathers, diamond towers, windmills, &c. . . . Now, easy tresses, the shining braid, the flowing ringlet confined by the *antique* comb, or bodkin, give graceful specimens of the simple taste of modern beauty. Nothing can correspond more elegantly with the untrammelled drapery of our newly-adopted classic raiment than this undecorated coiffure of nature.'[20]

The Mirror of the Graces, 1811

The quote above, though fulsome, suggests that the most distinctive development in Regency hairdressing, compared with the previous decades, was the reappearance of natural or naturalistic hair for both sexes – unpowdered, dressed close to the head or cropped (cut short), and with *wigs made to imitate real tresses. Natural hair was showcased in different ways from previous years, although there were many *hairpieces available to give nature a helping hand. Dyes and bleaches could also be deployed to improve upon what nature had endowed. In this section, male and female hair care and styling are addressed together. First comes a visual guide to women's hairstyles for every year between 1795 and 1820, and to men's hairstyles at intervals over the same period, before going into the glossary of relevant words. A section on Beauty and Hygiene, including cosmetics, follows.

Charles Woodward, 'A Dandy' (detail), 1818

WOMEN'S HAIR

> The auburn hair the ——— wears,
> Is her's [*sic*], and who'd have thought it;
> She swears 'tis hers, and true she swears,
> For I know where she bought it[21]

Regency women's hair was divided approximately from ear to ear into *front or short hair (also called the *toupee), and long *hind or back hair, which could reach the knees. The front hair was the site of innumerable hairstyling modes, often based around *curls and waves, appearing in almost every female image of the period. Because the front hair was shorter all over, it looked more like the front of a mullet than a modern fringe or bangs. Popular modern ideas of Regency ringlets have overshadowed the frequent use in the period of *braids, and *bands of straightened hair to create equally elegant styles. The alternative to long hair was the newly acceptable *crop, or short hair all over the head, seen a lot on children and in images of haircuts growing out on teenage young ladies. Women frequently wore *wigs in natural hair colours and added to their hair with *hairpieces, especially *fronts, a separate fringe of curls. As the *Book of Trades* put it in the 1806 edition, wigs and other ornamental decorations made of hair 'are now become so common, that few ladies, notwithstanding they possess the most beautiful hair, would be thought to be without false hair'.[22] Such articles could be made from their own hair, their daughter's or other female relative's, or bought for five shillings to five pounds per ounce, depending on quality and colour, from a hair merchant. The latter obtained their stock from women selling their hair, often imported from across Europe. The *Book of Trades* estimated that 'if we may judge from the splendid appearance of many shops in which ladies' wigs, braids, and curls are manufactured, no business is more flourishing or more profitable'.[23] Hairdressers could also be wig-makers, and part of their business was the cleaning and styling of wigs, for both sexes.

In an age with far fewer good-quality or large mirrors, gentry women usually relied on help from ladies' maids, female relatives and friends to dress their hair into the complicated styles. Professional hairdressers, always men, were common. They often visited at home to trim women's hair – recommended once a month to prevent split ends – and to create fashionable hairstyles. Another person could see and arrange the back of one's head with ease, where the focus of the coiffure often was. Generally – and vaguely – 'antique' Greek and Roman styles were popular. Curls were created with *curl-papers or could be bought separately; and hair was held up by *combs and *hairpins (J). There was a trend towards more centre-front parts from the mid-1810s. Adult women generally wore a *cap at home, so it was in *evening dress that hair inventiveness really shone. Looking at images and texts showing how flowers, real and *artificial, jewels including *pins (J) and *diadems (J), *bandeaux, *ribbons (T) and more were incorporated into hairstyles helps to bring the endless possibilities to mind.

Brushing hair vigorously – the proverbial hundred strokes a night for long female hair – did a lot of the action of washing to keep hair clean. Brushing helps distribute natural oils down the hair shafts and keeps it in condition. The linen or cotton *caps and *nightcaps women wore also helped absorb oil from the hair's surface. To wash the hair, women could first help remove any *powder, *pomade or *oil with a small-tooth comb. The washing solution could be soda (sodium carbonate) dissolved in water, or soap and water, though period sources frequently warn against the effects of harsh soap on the hair and recommend water alone.

Women's hair styles

Undone Hair

1795

1796

1797

1798

1799

1800

1801

1802

1803

1804

1805

1806

1807

1808

1809

1810

1811

1812
1813
1814
1815
1816
1817
1818
1819
1820

Men's hair styles

1798

1800

1802

1805

1808

1812

1816

1819

Full caption details for each of the women's and men's hairstyles can be found on pp. 243–4, in order of year

MEN'S HAIR

Men's natural hair re-appeared as a general fashion for the first time in centuries. The old obviously false powdered hair and grey horsehair *wigs of the previous century did not disappear completely, but became a sign of a profession, such as a doctor or lawyer, or simply looked archaic and old-fashioned. These are not represented in the images above but can be seen in some pictures throughout this book. Thanks to the *hair powder tax of 1795, classicism and finance together encouraged fashions from the late 1790s for cropped, curled, artfully dishevelled men's hairstyles modelled after antique notables and sculptures, with names to match. Men groomed themselves with cropped hairstyles à la *Titus, or in the *Brutus fashion, and kept their faces clean-shaven, with *whiskers appearing from the later 1800s, but never a *beard or stubble. If their own grown hair was not quite voluminous enough, or going grey, men could also choose natural-looking wigs. These can often be distinguished in portraits by a discrepancy between the colour of the sitter's hair and that of his eyebrows and side-whiskers.

The Whole Art of Dress, although published in 1830, offers a helpful insight in its recommendation that men trim their hair at least once a month (which was done at a barber's), and wash it once a fortnight in summer and once a month in winter. The washing should be done with water, 'hot as you can bear it; and if soap be used in winter, in summer it never should. Care should be taken in washing [the soap] well out, as it is pernicious in the extreme', meaning it can stick in the hair unless washed out well or with a vinegar or other acidic rinse.[24] As with women's hair, condition and oil distribution was helped by brushing vigorously every day, first with a hard brush, and then with a soft brush. Men also wore *nightcaps (M) which helped absorb oils. If a gentleman had a valet, the servant helped arrange the hair each day, and applied *pomades and preparations.

Valets would also lay out a man's shaving equipment, and sometimes shave him. It was an operation requiring skill and experience, both to complete and to maintain the tools. A straight-edge razor was sharpened on a razor-strap or strop to create a good, regular cutting edge. Then came a pre-wash of the face, and a lather made using a good-quality, mild *shaving soap, or *shaving powder applied with a brush; or these were applied to the face and then raised to a lather with the hands. Increasingly, men started shaving themselves during this period. Visiting a barber, however, was the traditional option.

GLOSSARY

back hair *See* *hind hair.

bands Smooth, straight sections of hair, as opposed to curls, created by arranging the *front hair, or by wrapping the long *hind hair around the head.

John Wesley Jarvis (attrib.), Portrait of Mrs James Lawrence, *c.1810*

beard Beards were entirely out of fashion at this period, even for working men. A notable exception that proves the rule is the eccentric dandy Charles Stanhope, until 1829 Viscount Petersham, who affected a small, pointed beard to accentuate his physical resemblance to Henri IV, king of France between 1589 and 1610. *See also* *whiskers.

bouffant A kind of *hairpiece.

braid A plait of *hind hair, used decoratively in the hairstyle; or a separate *hairpiece in the form of a plait.

John Downman, Mrs Coade, *1806*

Brutus [*à la Brutus*] A male dishevelled, highly curled, *cropped hairstyle or *wig style, named after short Roman-type hairstyles worn by actor Jacques-Marie Boutet de Monvel playing Lucius Junius Brutus in a revival of Voltaire's play *Brutus*, performed during the French Revolution on 30 May 1791, the thirteenth anniversary of the writer's death. *See also* *Titus.

comb [haircomb] Functional and decorative ornament of various sizes with two or more prongs or teeth for styling and arranging women's hair, made from shell, tortoiseshell, ivory, horn, bone, metal (sometimes bejewelled), and other materials. *Diadems (J) comprised a *frontlet attached to a comb.

John Hazlitt, Mrs John Hazlitt Reading, *c.1795–1800*

crop A hairstyle for men and women, in which the hair was cut short or close to the head, leaving no long hair at the back. It came from French Revolutionary fashions in the 1790s, but was soon widely adopted, either in the natural hair or as a *wig. Cutting the hair short was thought to have some health benefits, and it was more convenient for wearing under a wig. *See also* *Brutus, *Titus.

'Half Dress', September 1816

curl-paper A piece of soft paper in which hair is twisted up for some time, to give it a curl when the paper is taken out. They were bought in quires at a stationer's. Both women and men used curl-papers, including Lord Byron.

curls The preferred description of curled hair, real or a hairpiece, rather than ringlets, or ringlet curls (although these appear in some texts). Women could buy 'curls for behind', showing on the nape of the neck, and 'drop curls' as single ringlets to add to their coiffures.

front A *hairpiece or 'kind of semiwig'[25] imitating a fringe as a row of ringlets sewn to a tape and tied around the head, to be worn at the front of a woman's head, sometimes made of a woman's own hair, or her daughter's. Part of the appeal of *turbans for older women was that they covered the real hair completely, allowing a visible front to peep out from underneath and give the illusion of ungreyed hair.

front hair The hair cut shorter on the front half of women's heads down to the ears, contrasting with the long *hind hair; often styled into *curls or waves.

'Costume Parisien', no. 1500 (detail), 1815

hair powder White powder made from ground wheat or rice, used to set and colour hair and *wigs, and to impart a greyish appearance. In 1795 'an annual tax of one guinea was laid upon all persons who should in future wear hair powder'[26] to raise money for the British government and in response to a bad wheat harvest, which lessened the fashion, and the following years saw an almost complete decline in the use of powder by 1820.

hair ribbon A ribbon with at least one dull, matte surface, the better to grip the hair and not slide out.

hairpiece An ornamental decoration made of hair, sometimes called 'ornamental hair'; less than a full *wig, also called a semi-wig. *See also* *bouffant, *curl, *front, *tete, *toupee.

hind hair [back hair] The long hair grown on the back half of women's heads, sometimes reaching the knees, used for creating hairstyles and contrasting with the short *front hair.

moustache [moustachio, mustache, mustachio] *See* *whiskers.

ornamental hair *See* *hairpieces.

peruke An older word for *wig, falling out of use by the 1810s.

powder For hair, *see* *hair powder. For the face, *see* *face powder, and for the body *see* *powder, both under Beauty and Hygiene (see p. 152).

sideburns *See* *whiskers.

side-whiskers *See* *whiskers.

tete A full *wig or *hairpiece. French for 'head' (*tête*).

Titus [*à la Titus, coiffure à la Titus*] A male and female dishevelled, loosely curled, *cropped hairstyle or *wig style with the hair dressed towards and covering the forehead, named after the wildly popular short Roman-type hairstyle worn by François-Joseph Talma in a revival of Voltaire's play *Brutus*, performed in Paris during the French Revolution on 30 May 1791, the thirteenth anniversary of the writer's death. *See also* *Brutus.

toupee The front part of the hair; *front hair.

whiskers (1) An all-purpose, interchangeable term for the sideburns and/or moustache. Generally, only military men, especially those in Hussar and Light Dragoon regiments, wore a moustache. (2) Side-whiskers or sideburns, which started to become popular for young men around 1806 in Britain and during the 1810s, the whiskers extended down the cheek, and were grown longer. False whiskers were available.

wig [wigg] A head-covering *hairpiece worn by men and women, made from human hair, horsehair or vegetable imitations of hair, attached to a base of linen or silk fabric, or tapes, called the *cawl (caul). Besides changing the appearance of the hair, they were a warm head garment. Wigs were an ongoing expense, thanks to the upkeep of professional washing, dressing and combing out.

WOMEN: during this period, women's wigs were always of a natural pigmented hair colour, often their own after it was cut off for a *crop, not grey, white or powdered. Women frequently used wigs and hairpieces to cover up greying hair and keep their original colour into later life, or to change their hair colour without dyeing it. Some older women shaved their head and used their own hair to make the wig, or they might use their daughter's hair.

MEN: after *hair powder use diminished in 1795–1800, men also wore more natural-coloured wigs, in their own hair colour or a different one. Eighteenth-century-style white or grey horsehair wigs continued in some use, but denoted being old and out of fashion, and were acceptable only for professional or occupational reasons, such as for clergymen, the legal profession and doctors of law.

James Lonsdale, Joseph Nollekens, *c.1818*

BEAUTY AND HYGIENE

A good complexion was seen as the foundation of all female beauty, and many pages of recipes and advice were dedicated to achieving this, mostly summarised as 'wash your face well' with a good *soap, and the use of floral *waters, primarily rose and lavender, which appear the most frequently in contemporary account books. Men also were encouraged to wash their faces well to establish a good complexion. *Creams were used to cleanse the face and act as moisturisers, as were *balms, and scented *oils, also used on the hair for gloss and condition. Bleaches and depilatory creams for the face and arms were advertised, though it is hard to know how often they were used, and they appear to have contained poisonous arsenic. Then, as now, advertisers promised miracles in a jar.

Regency women did wear some cosmetics. We know this because of many period sources complaining that they are, or that they are wearing them too obviously. The new natural aesthetics of the 1790s meant cosmetic use was subtler and less artificial than the earlier eighteenth-century practices, but, like *wigs, they changed form rather than disappearing completely. A woman who used cosmetics aimed for a 'no makeup makeup', whereby her looks were enhanced with no perceptible use of substances. *Rouge was the only truly acceptable genteel cosmetic, but women were expected to use it delicately. The colour intensity and placement of rouge was the subject of much discussion at the time, and its 'overuse' attracted misogynistic and xenophobic critiques, with the French being particularly attacked.

Paint or enamel was the term for a base layer, usually white, painted over the skin to make it paler in line with the dominant white European beauty ideals. It was seen as a sign of vanity, easily abused and detected, and noted for its danger to health, as the finest-quality paint contained white lead which the skin absorbed. This imparted a delicate, pearlescent quality to the skin, filling in minor blemishes and creating a very smooth surface, in a way no modern foundation made with safe ingredients has yet replicated. Lesser-quality paint without lead was thicker and more obvious. Particularly dedicated paint users sometimes painted blue veins onto the surface to enhance the 'natural' illusion. *Face powder was more acceptable as, if discreet, it absorbed oil and created a matte effect without affecting skin tone, although pearl powder had a slight sheen. Some women pencilled or stained their eyebrows darker, and also used red-tinted *lip salves to enhance their lips. Plain salves were recommended for chapped lips.

Books also repeatedly stress the importance of cleanliness of person and clothing to beauty, health and virtue. Ears and nails were recommended to be cleaned daily upon rising, along with the teeth and mouth. This was achieved by brushing the teeth using a toothbrush or cloth, with salt water, tooth powders, charcoal or other cleansing substances; and cleaning the tongue 'with a small piece of whalebone, or with a sage leaf'.[27] Teeth were cleaned again at night.

Middle- and upper-class people washed daily, usually in the morning in their bedroom, using a washbasin and sponge or a 'hard and dry linen cloth',[28] and cold, luke-warm or hot water brought in by a servant. Soap was optional, as the friction from a cloth was an effective exfoliant. More frequent washing of the face, hands and feet was recommended, preferably twice a day. People less often took full baths, due to the time and effort required to heat and transport large quantities of water, before the arrival of piped running water. Texts distinguish carefully between cold, cool, tepid, warm and hot baths; those that fully immerse the bather, or only the lower half (a hip bath); shower baths, where the water descended from an apparatus above; and foot baths. The judicious application of these was considered a health measure, and much concern was paid to being neither too cool nor too hot. Tepid baths were recommended for general cleanliness. However, going into the sea, a river or lake was also considered bathing, and people had a surprising enthusiasm for cold water immersion.

I have found no recipes or advice for underarm deodorant substances in this period. Instead, the main concerns about armpit perspiration were that the moisture was held next to the body and could potentially cause illness through dampness. Body odour was mentioned as only a problem for some people. This was also the case with foot odour, to which there are more references in sources. The remedy for this was frequent washing, changing *stockings often, and paying attention to what material they were made of. Clothing was an important part of keeping a clean person. The reason people wore linen or cotton undergarments such as *shirts, *shifts and *drawers next to the skin was that they were washable and protected less washable outer clothing from any oils and sweat from the body, like a lining. Changing soiled or damp linens and stockings frequently was part of cleanliness and hygiene practices. Screen productions showing women wearing *corsets or *stays over bare skin (in any period of history) are therefore illogical. No Regency woman would have worn the expensive, complex garment without the textile buffer underneath, especially for a garment that would rub the skin otherwise – like wearing shoes without stockings.

All the products below have been found in Regency magazine advertisements, texts or account books. Books of domestic or household advice are another good source for information on health and beauty products. Many recommendations and recipes need to be assessed carefully for their accuracy, to clear away the advertising spiels and exaggerated claims of efficacy.

GLOSSARY

balm A semi-solid ointment made from waxes and oils.

cream An oil and/or wax emulsified with water: cold cream, cream of roses, cream of almonds, cream *des sultanas*.

face powder Powder made from ground pearls, rice or wheat.

Gowland's Lotion A cleanser and kind of peel to remove freckles, tanning and skin eruptions, made from an emulsion of the milk of bitter and sweet almonds, plus bichloride of mercury, therefore with harmful side effects. Originally invented by John Gowland in the mid eighteenth century, and famous now from Sir Walter Elliot's recommendation in Jane Austen's novel *Persuasion* (1817).

hair oil Macassar oil or bear's grease for men, rubbed into the roots and brushed out well.

lip salve A *balm used to soften and moisturise the lips, and, if tinted, to colour them.

lozenges In floral (especially rose) or strong flavours such as camphor, to sweeten the breath.

oil 'Antique' and infused oils of carnations, jasmine, roses, violet, orris, musk, lemon, thyme, rosemary.

paint [enamel] A base layer, usually white, painted over women's facial skin to make it paler and smoother. The most effective paint used dangerous white lead to create a smooth, pearlescent quality.

perfume [scent] Egyptian mignonette, palmyrene violet, almond, Ceylon bandana, eau de Cologne.

pomade [pomatum] A greasy, waxy or water-based substance used to style hair.

powder Mignonette powders, Pears' botanic white imperial powder for the complexion.

refreshing salts [smelling salts, eau de luce] Pungently scented salts of ammonia (*sal ammoniac*) to revive after a shock, to help ease a headache, or to apply to insect bites.

rouge Red-coloured powder or liquid used to impart a blush to female cheeks. Products included Pears' almond bloom, Riggs' liquid bloom and other liquid vegetable rouges, and carmine powder. Paler complexions were advised to tone down rouge with face powder.

William Beechey, Frances Elizabeth Addington, *c.1805*

shaving paste A ready-made preparation which lathered quickly and easily.

shaving powder Powder made from small soap flakes.

shaving soap Soap made with ingredients to create a higher degree of lather.

soap Almond soap, Bandana soap, Indian washing cakes, Royal Abyssinian flower soap, Italian or Naples soap, olive soap, otto of rose soap, palm oil and Windsor soaps, generally called toilet soaps, transparent soap.

water A scented tonic and face wash, made by infusing or distilling: lavender water, rose water, milk of roses, honey waters.

JEWELLERY

'Elegant dressing is not found in expense; money without judgment may load, but never can adorn. You may show profusion without grace: you may cover a neck with pearls, a head with jewels, hands and arms with rings, bracelets and trinkets, and yet produce no effect, but having emptied some merchant's counter upon your person.'[29]

The Mirror of the Graces, 1811

This chapter focuses on the styles and forms of Regency jewellery fashionable at the time, with some explanations for objects no longer in use, less common, or with a different purpose compared to the present day. Male and female examples are combined.

Overall, from the 1790s jewellery styles became lighter and finer. The design focus was often on the past. Classical, antique styles were popular, inspired by Ancient Greece, Rome and Egypt, with jewellers often imitating archaeological pieces. Some jewellery even incorporated original antique pieces such as *cameos and *intaglios. The medieval and Renaissance periods also provided inspiration, as did a renewed interest in naturalistic forms sparked by emerging Romanticism. Predominant motifs in jewellery of all types included: acanthus leaves, Apollo's lyre, birds, butterflies, crescent moons, Cupid's arrows, ears of corn, feathers, Greek keys, laurel wreaths and leaves, Mercury's caduceus, naturalistic flowers, olive leaves, palmettes, rosettes, scrolls and clusters, stars, urns and vine leaves.

A key development in jewellery in the late eighteenth century was the 'brilliant' cut with multiple facets that increased the sparkle of diamonds, which came to dominate fine jewellery. *Brilliants, as they

Sir Thomas Lawrence, Mrs Siddons, *1804, depicting a suite of jewellery*

were called, were usually set in open mounts (*à jour*) with no backs, which allowed the light to shine through the stone. Lesser stones continued to be set in closed mounts. Because of its high intrinsic value, little original diamond jewellery survives. Owners frequently had the gems re-set into more fashionable designs, especially upon marriage, when the bride might inherit family pieces that needed updating. More gems changed hands and were re-set in Britain as refugees and émigrés fleeing the French Revolution sold their jewellery to realise its value. Expensive jewellery was often modular: it could be recombined to make different pieces. A *rivière could convert into two *bracelets. Parts of an *aigrette could be inserted into a base to form a *tiara. The drops of long *earrings could detach to leave only a cluster at the ear. Because of the enduring value and strength of jewellery, more survives in good condition than textile items.

Everyday Regency jewellery was relatively modest in nature. Delicate *chains, *necklaces, *rings, bracelets and other accessories complemented men and women alike. However, fewer of these trinkets survive, being less durable and valuable. Images then become richer sources for researching what such pieces looked like and how they were worn.

MATERIALS OF JEWELLERY

precious stones Diamond, emerald, ruby, sapphire.

semi-precious stones Amethyst, aquamarine, chrysoberyl, chrysolite, citrine, garnet, opal, topaz, tourmaline, turquoise.

hardstones Agate, bloodstone, chrysoprase, red and white cornelian, lapis lazuli, malachite, rock crystal, sardonyx.

natural materials Amber, coral, ivory, jet, pearls, seed pearls.

metals Gold, iron, pinchbeck (copper and zinc alloy), platinum, silver, steel.

GLOSSARY

aigrette A hair or *headwear ornament designed to hold or depict feathers, usually bejewelled and sometimes mounted as a *trembler. Also worn as part of male military dress. French for 'egret', a heron with distinctive tail feathers.

Pinchbeck aigrette in the form of a plume of feathers tied with a disc of carnelian, c.1815

armlet A *bracelet worn on the upper forearm or above the elbow, sometimes in a matched set with wrist bracelets.

Arthur William Devis, Harriet Leonard Bull, *c.1810*

bracelet A flexible link-formed wrist band, as opposed to a bangle, which is rigid. Bracelets were often owned and worn in pairs (*en suite*), including over gloves and cuffs. 'Elastic ribbon' bracelets had fine springs concealed inside.

Gold bracelet, set with coloured glass plaques, c.1815

brilliant (1) A diamond of the finest cut and brilliancy. (2) Any gemstone 'brilliant' cut with multiple facets to increase its sparkle.

brooch [broach] An ornamental piece of jewellery with a pin (with or without a clasp or hook) used as decoration for, or to join or affix, parts of male and female clothing or accessories, including *shirt fronts, *neck-handkerchiefs, *gowns, *pelisse fronts, *veils, *cloaks and *scarves, or used as decoration for *headwear, or worn as hair adornment. The most typical figurative shapes were sunbursts, stars, crescents, ribbon bows, and sprays of leaves.

Sir Thomas Lawrence, Unknown sitter (formerly called Miss Lamb), c.*1818–21*

buckle Used as closure for male shoe straps for *court dress, breeches cuffs, the back of *stocks, and, for women, on belts. The fitting with teeth which grasps the fabric or leather is called the chape. When decorative or with gemstones, a form of jewellery.

button Large *coat and smaller decorated *waistcoat buttons made from precious metals, gilt, gems, *enamel or *cut steel counted as jewellery, and were made in sets for men's *court dress (M), kept in cases like other precious adornments. For the non-jewellery items, *see* *button (T).

Boxed set of men's cut and polished steel waistcoat and coat buttons, 1800–20

cameo A hardstone on which a design is cut in three-dimensional relief, generally figurative of a profile or a figure. Traditional stones included sardonyx, cornelian, chalcedony, jasper and agate; shell was also used. The fashion for cameos was inspired by travel to Italy, and jewellery might incorporate genuine antique examples.

Necklace with shell cameos including cupids and pairs of doves, missing a pendant, Italy, c.1810

cannetille Gold filigree wire work.

A pink topaz and gold cannetille suite, comprising necklace, bracelet, brooch and earrings, c.1800

chain, neck chain A plain chain, made to support a *pendant, *watch, *eye glass, *miniature or other trinkets, as opposed to a *necklace which was decorative in its own right.

clasp A jewellery or belt closure with two parts that hook together for fastening.

cresting The standing part of a *tiara or hair *comb.

cross The most popular design of *pendant or *brooch, in the Latin, Greek or Maltese shape, often set with stones, worn hanging from a *necklace, *chain or *ribbon (T).

Topaz cross on a gold chain once belonging to Jane or Cassandra Austen, 1801

cut steel [cut-steel] Steel cut, faceted and polished to create shine and sparkle.

demi-parure A smaller *parure set comprising as little as two or three pieces – necklace and earrings, possibly with a brooch.

diadem [diadem comb] A crown-like jewelled ribbon or metal band-style head ornament worn across the brow, attached by a *comb and held at each end by hairpins, often in imitation of Ancient Greek or Roman styles.

earring [ear-ring] Worn only by women, popular styles were single drops, long drops, hoops, and pear drop shapes. Earrings were worn for *dress and *undress, the difference being that less valuable materials were worn during the day, and more valuable in the evening.

'Evening Dress', July 1819

en tremblant *See* *trembler.

enamel Decorative coating made from powdered glass that is fused to a metal base. In 1775 a London jeweller perfected a kind of royal blue enamel, and the coloured material proliferated afterwards in jewellery.

eye glass *See* *quizzing glass.

eye miniature [lover's eye] A short-lived fashion from the 1780s to about 1820 of a loved one's eye painted on ivory, like a *miniature, set in a *locket, medallion, *pendant, *brooch or other object, and given as a keepsake or *memorial piece, to remind the recipient of love and affection.

Gold locket set with pearls, enclosing an eye painted on ivory, the back set with hair and pearls, c.1800

Jean-Auguste-Dominique Ingres, Admiral Sir Fleetwood Broughton Reynolds Pellew, *1817*

fob [fob chain] Originally a small pocket in the waistband of the breeches, used for carrying a watch, money, or other valuables (*see* *fob [M]). From this usage, the word became: (1) used as a shorthand for small decorative or functional objects carried in or attached to the fob pocket by a chain, strap or ribbon, such as a *fob seal or *fob watch; (2) a synonym for the attaching length itself as fob, or fob chain, the latter sometimes called a *watch chain; (3) a synonym for a fob seal.

fob seal A small decorative seal or signet ring used for imprinting sealing wax, attached to a *watch chain or a *fob (M and J). Sometimes also shortened to 'fob'.

Gold fob seal with citrine, one face with an intaglio depicting the Battle of Trafalgar (1805), c.1815–20

fob watch A small watch that fitted in the *fob pocket (M), attached by a *fob chain or *watch chain.

frontlet The decorative part of a *diadem comb mount. One *comb could have several frontlets.

hair jewellery Human hair from loved ones set into jewellery, or braided and plaited into jewellery structures such as *necklaces and *bracelets; often but not always *memorial.

Gold brooch set with amethysts and seed pearls enclosing plaited hair, early nineteenth century

hairpin A single- or double-pronged implement for securing a hairstyle or embellishing the hair, sometimes with decoration or a *pendant.

harlequin A description for jewellery combining different-coloured stones in one piece.

intaglio A decorative engraving into hardstone; the reverse of a *cameo, which was in relief.

locket A small case opening on hinges, frequently made as a *pendant, often containing a sentimental memento such as a *miniature portrait or lock of hair.

lorgnette A pair of eye glasses held in the hand, usually with a long decorative handle.

lover's eye *See* *eye miniature.

memorial jewellery Pieces of jewellery, usually rings or brooches, made to commemorate a deceased loved one, often funded by money left in the person's will. Rings often incorporated funerary imagery such as urns, broken pillars, plinths, obelisks, weeping willows, cherubs, angels and mourning figures, or were made from black or white *enamel. *Hair jewellery was often a form of memorial.

Clockwise from top: locket, 1775–1800; pendant, 1775–1800; locket, c.1800; locket, 1775–1800

Mather Brown, Susannah Jones (Mrs Alban Thomas Gwynne), *wearing a miniature, c.1810*

miniature [miniature portrait] A small-scale oval, circular or rectangular portrait of a loved one, executed with delicacy in watercolour or gouache on ivory, sometimes vellum or paper, set into a case or other support; either separate, or as part of *rings, *studs, *bracelets and *lockets, the latter worn on a woman's *girdle, or around the neck.

mourning jewellery *See* *memorial jewellery.

necklace Jewellery adornment intended for wear around the neck in its own right, contrasting with a *chain which supported other items. Fashionable styles included chokers, single and multiple strands, chains with *cameos or *intaglios set into them, and *rivières.

Cut-steel necklace, early 19th century

opaline glass [opal paste] A faux gem made of glass with a pale, variegated, milky appearance, tinged pink or blue by setting the paste over coloured foil.

parure A group of matching jewellery items of uniform design, made as a set, featuring precious or semi-precious stones, comprising up to as many as sixteen individual pieces, sometimes referred to as a 'suite', or *en suite*, and stored in a fabric-lined case. A full parure could include a *necklace, *earrings, hair ornaments including a *comb, *tiara or *diadem, *dress ornaments such as bows, a set of *buttons, a waist *buckle, a pair of *bracelets, a *pendant and *brooches. *See also* *demi-parure.

Parure with scenes of Rome in micro-mosaics, set in gold, comprising earrings, necklace, bracelets, pendant and brooches, 1800–25

paste A form of glass invented by Georges-Frédéric Strass around 1720, made hard and durable by the addition of lead oxide to flint glass, allowing paste to be cut and shaped like the gemstones it imitated. Paste stones were valuable in their own right and could be foiled or coated at the back with a thin leaf of silver or coloured metals to increase their brilliancy.

pendant A decorative piece with a loop or hook at the top to hang off a *chain, *necklace or *rivière.

pin A single prong or spike, usually with an ornamental end, used for joining and decorating clothing, or affixing *handkerchiefs, *neckerchiefs, *scarves, and other small textile accessories. *See also* *hairpin.

quizzing glass [eye glass, quizzer] A single portable magnifying, corrective or non-functional glass lens on a decorative, usually metal or bone handle which was held up to the eye to 'quiz' something in view; worn by men and women, on the end of a long ribbon or *chain around the neck or at the waist. A single eye glass was often used in place of a pair of spectacles.

'Morning Dress' (detail), July 1814

ring A vast range of styles of rings were fashionable, in every metal: *signet, set with *cameos, ivory scenes, *miniature portraits. Most common was the half-hoop set with a single row or double rows of gemstones. Men and women wore rings; women could wear multiple rings on one finger or hand.

rivière A necklace comprising gemstones of the same type, evenly sized or graduating in size. Some rivières included a small hinged loop or loops that allowed a matching *pendant, often a *cross, to be suspended. They could also be worn in the hair.

A faceted garnet rivière necklace, c.1800

seal A decorative engraved stamp of metal or other hard material, especially hardstone, used to make an impression upon wax of the design it carries; often attached to a *fob chain. *See also* *fob seal and *signet ring.

shirt-brooch *See* *brooch.

signet ring A finger ring, usually worn by men, featuring a *seal, lettering or a design engraved in it.

stud Like a cufflink, for fastening cuffs and shirt fronts.

suite *See* *parure.

tiara A crown-like jewelled metal band-style head ornament, attached by hairpins or a ribbon; different from a *diadem, which attached with a *comb. Tiaras were only worn by married women.

transparent A stone or *paste set without a foil back, leaving it clear.

trembler [*en tremblant*] Any ornament, extended on a wire or a spring, that shakes with movement.

watch [pocket-watch] A small portable timepiece used by men and women, either open-faced or in decorative cases, chased, engraved, enamelled, or in an ornamental shape. Men's watches were kept in the pocket of their waistcoat or breeches, hanging from *watch-chains or *fobs. Women attached watches to hooks or *chains at the waist, or wore them over the bust on a *chain. Women and men could use the same style of watch, though those made for women tended to be smaller; people also distinguished between their 'best' and 'common', or everyday, watch. *See also* *fob watch.

Louis Recordon, a yellow gold open-faced repeating watch, London, 1807

watch chain [watch string] Any *chain or *fob used to attach a *watch to a gentleman's pocket, or a lady's *gown, for security and ease of use. Male watch chains could be decorative pieces of jewellery, designed to show from under the waistcoat. In addition to a watch, the watch chain could also support the watch key, a *fob seal, and other small accessory items.

Wedgwood jewellery Jewellery made from Wedgwood jasperware ceramics, with a soft matte finish, in the form of plaques and beads set into metals.

Enamelled gold fob chain, set with pearls, with watch key and seal attached, c.1800

Blue, green and black Wedgwood jasperware beads, with a gold clasp, early 19th century

TEXTILES
&
TRIMMINGS

1
2
3
ICH
DIEN
March 1809.
The Repository
Of Arts, Literature, Commerce, Manufactures, Fashion, and Politics.
Manufacturers, Factors, and Wholesale Dealers in Fancy Goods that come within the scope of this Plan, are requested to send Patterns of such new Articles as they come out, and if the requisites of Novelty, Fashion, and Elegance are united, the quantity necessary for this Magazine will be ordered. R. Ackermann, 101, Strand, London.

'. . . human nature is a Monmouth-street, a collection of suits . . . – silk, gauze, and frivolity – leather and prunella, goats hair and gold lace. . . . What makes all the young ladies "fall in love" with him? – It is the red coat. The silk and the muslin fall in love with the scarlet and the lace; they elope together to Gretna Green.'[30]

'On Fashions', *The London Magazine*, 1825

The material components of clothing and accessories were essential to dress. Textiles, leather, fur, and all sorts of haberdashery and trimmings were a large part of how Regency people understood clothes. Because everything was sewn by hand, by professional tailors and dressmakers, or people at home who had done it all their lives, there was an intimate tactile knowledge of what fabrics did, and how they behaved and performed; their temperature-regulating qualities, and how well they would wash, or wear, or wear out. For the Regency lady perusing a fashion magazine, there was an inherent difference between whether the pretty white gown she was looking at a picture of was a *cambric or a *jaconet muslin, if it was *japanned or *tamboured, or trimmed with hand- or machine-made *lace. Her husband was equally concerned about whether his new *Hessian boots were made of calf or *Spanish leather, and his glossy new *riding coat from *superfine or *kerseymere wool fabrics. These material qualities were also equally important to people simply viewing fashion, because subtle differences imparted lots of knowledge to the observers as to class, status, wealth, taste, and all the other nuances of dressed display.

Fabric samples: 1. Anglo-Merino cloth; 2. Queen's silk; 3. Satin twilled silk; 4. Persian double silk, March 1809

The proliferation of new fabrics created during the Regency period, and the increased range of their qualities and varieties, demanded from consumers new kinds of what scholars call 'material literacy' – the ability to 'read' fabrics. Fine *muslins, for instance, were increasingly distinguished between handwoven Indian and machine-woven British products – differences that Henry Tilney is famously able to identify in Jane Austen's novel *Northanger Abbey*.[31] Improvements to the quality of British muslins allowed them to compete with imported textiles by the early nineteenth century. *Cotton fabrics in general increased in quality and quantity, requiring consumers to understand not only the quality of the fibres and weave, but also the colour-fastness of their printed patterns.

Industrial innovations were revolutionising spinning and weaving from the 1760s, including machines for mass-manufacturing lace. The delicate textile required huge amounts of skill, labour and time, and was correspondingly expensive. Thomas Taylor patented a point net machine in 1778 which created a hexagonal net from loops, adapted from knitting machines. The Hayne brothers improved upon this to produce double-press point net. Their big innovation was to create a net that did not run when cut, unlike the original single point net looped from one thread which unravelled easily. This success stimulated further lace-making innovations from other inventors during the 1790s. Taylor's patent (and others) gave rise to the common name 'patent net' or 'patent lace' for these looped net productions, which appears throughout Regency fashion commentary. One of the problems with *patent net was its need to be stiffened with gum arabic or similar substances to maintain the hexagonal ground appearance. Finally, John Heathcoat's 1808 invention of a net-making machine that exactly reproduced the twist-net (diamond-shaped) ground of lace handmade using bobbins, in cotton or silk, was perfected in 1809 (although his work built on innovations in other existing machines). Other advances followed, bringing further technological innovations to the marketplace. Airy silk *gauzes, *tulles, *bobbin nets and cheaper patent nets appear frequently in surviving garments in the 1810s. Gowns using diaphanous net textiles, in particular, needed petticoats to wear under them, such as full underdresses called *slips made of white or coloured silk. Slips could affect the appearance of the gown's outer colour. A net dress's fragile tensile strength also called for construction techniques that provided structural integrity along seams and stress or tension points, to avoid any tearing during wear. Gauzy fabrics increased in gowns from about 1814, at the same time as longer *stays became popular that would afford a firmer under-shape to reduce the strain of physical movement on the external fabric.

Rudolph Ackermann's monthly magazine *The Repository of Arts* called attention to the central importance of how people understood textiles by including fabric samples in its pages, as seen on page 174, and many more of which are reproduced in the following entries. The quality of the fabric needed to be felt to be valued, and for modern readers these samples are an excellent resource for matching textile names to what the material looked like. In other magazines that shared information on fashion, descriptions accompanying engraved fashion plates detailed the images' specific weaves, fibres, colours and trimmings, tapping into the reader's existing material literacy as an essential part of bringing the image to life. To truly understand the qualities of a dress in a fashion plate, one needs to know its component fabrics and their full colour ranges by reading the accompanying description. The watercolour washes added to the engravings can give the impression of paler hues than were necessarily the case for the real fabrics, which were often vivid.

The account books of Regency women further highlight the importance to them of haberdashery and trimmings as an essential part of making fashion. The cost of all the components of an ensemble was decipherable to any observer with a precise, informed eye, combining material and economic literacy. Contemporary sources and surviving garments repeatedly distinguish between garment and trimmings as separate aspects of fashionable dress. Dressmaking was a task of two halves: foundation structures, and surface embellishment. The rapid increase in trimmings and handwork applied to the base gown and other garments remains an under-appreciated element in Regency dressmaking. This was a transitional period, when the production of textile and haberdashery items was becoming increasingly mechanised; these developments both increased the variety of goods and made them more readily and cheaply available. 'Trimming' as a verb or noun is as ambiguous as 'dress', so items found in Regency makers' bills and accounts could either refer to the task of applying the decoration or to the decoration that is being applied.

There is a distinct increase in haberdashery and trimmings on gowns after 1815. These trimmings put 'fashion' onto the foundation garment structure, while the foundation itself became redefined and multi-layered. Applying trimmings to textiles could take as long as (or, indeed, longer than) sewing the thing itself, with needlework ranging from quick, large stitches to complicated precise or repetitive sewing, to make a decorative surface with applied trimmings. Trimming labour added extra value to the economic worth of clothing's material components. The fashion from the late 1810s for *rouleau decoration – narrow bias-cut tubes made of the main gown fabric and applied in decorative patterns – required even more labour and fabric investment than most trimmings, as dressmakers complained. By about 1818 it was possible to confect a gown which consisted almost entirely of trimmings, using gauze, net, *blonde lace, bias strips, *ribbon leaves and *flowers, and *cartisane.

The account book of London widow and heiress Mrs Mary Topham (*c.*1755–1825) created between the years 1810 and 1825 illuminates a fuller picture of the costs involved in making fashion.[32] Her accounts show that extras, trimmings and accessories such as lace, flowers, ribbons, pins, fringing, *shoe binding and roses (*rosettes [F]), the braids *gimp and *galloon, *cord, tape, wadding and *buttons formed 47 per cent of the quantity of textiles and clothing-related items bought by her between 1811 and 1825, although fabrics were a greater cost. Ribbons, in particular, form the overwhelming majority of her purchases – at around 42 per cent of the haberdashery, or around 20 per cent of the total number of textile items, bought in every colour, width and quality on a weekly basis throughout the accounting period. Often they come after a set of fabrics for a named garment, such as a bonnet or pelisse, showing us how ribbons were an essential part of making fashionable dress. Even where trimmings might not have increased sewing time overall, they were always an extra expense.

The ability to construct a gown mostly of trimmings over textiles was a significant change from even the lightest muslin gowns of *c.*1800. Then, and through the early 1810s, many fashionable muslins came already *sprigged, spotted, tamboured or embroidered, either through the work of Indian craftspeople using *chikan* and *do-rukha* techniques before export to Britain, or in imitation of them (see the entry for *muslin). The decorative labour was already sewn into the cost of the uncut gown length before purchase, and had often been worked in a different country. By the 1820s, the effort of decorative labour had largely transferred to the fashioning of the gown after it was made, by British women – a quicker way to respond to fashionable change and styling than relying on a textile purchased with its decoration already sewn or woven into the fabric. The material and economic value of textiles and trimmings, although obvious to contemporary observers, has often become almost invisible to us now, a distant second to their decorative value.

Paying close attention to textiles and trimmings is a way to better understand surviving objects, to recreate or catalogue them more accurately, and to know how these garments functioned in their time. In the following glossary, I have left out fabrics that, while common, were not used for clothing and accessories, and have given the definition as closely as I can to how people at the time would have understood it. Names and meanings change over the decades, with some having other definitions even by the later nineteenth century, so there are notes when a material is now better known by a different name. The textile images here, except where illustrating a common type such as muslin, are as far as possible given from period sources where they are identified as such.

GLOSSARY

alamode A light glossy silk, typically black in colour, like a glossed *taffeta.

Alençon point [Alençon lace, *point d'Alençon*] A type of expensive handmade *point lace made by embroidering pattern motifs on a mesh ground using raised outlines of buttonhole stitches and decorative fillings.

Linen Alençon point border, 1790s

alepine [alepin, aleppine, allipeen, alapeen] A fine four-end (each weft thread passing over four warp threads) *twill fabric woven from a mixture of wool and silk or *mohair and cotton. Similar to *bombazine.

alpaca A cloth made from the fine, silky wool of the alpaca (*Lama pacos*), smaller than a llama.

angora [angola] Any textile made from the wool of the Angora goat (*Capra aegagrus hircus*). The variation 'angola' is a misspelling and has no connection with the African country of Angola.

atlas A rich silk-satin with gold or silver threads in the weave creating the pattern, often flowers or stripes. The wedding dress of Princess Charlotte of Wales (1796–1817) was made from silver and white atlas.

Mrs Triaud, wedding ensemble made for Princess Charlotte of Wales, 1816

baize [baise, bays, bayes] A cheap, coarse, open, plain-weave woollen cloth which was made in many colours, often with a *worsted warp and woollen weft. It was used for trousers, aprons, petticoats, jackets and gowns, and for lining clothes, and was especially popular for poorer, active and labouring people's dress. Commonly 1½ (137 cm), 1¾ (160 cm) or 2 (183 cm) yards wide. The nap could be *friezed.

Textile samples of baizes, 1800–25

baleen [baleine] *See* *whalebone.

barragan [baragan, barracan, barragon] A *worsted or woollen cloth, like a *camlet but coarser. The name is of Spanish origin.

batiste (Fr.) (1) *Cambric. (2) A fine linen cloth from Flanders or Picardy. Both types of cloth were popular for *morning gowns. It came in at least three qualities – very thin, less thin, and one resembling the texture of *Holland, so called Holland batiste.

bearskin [bear-skin] A thick, coarse woollen cloth, used for outerwear. Not to be confused with genuine bear *fur.

Textile samples of bearskins, late eighteenth century

beaver (1) **[beaver cloth]** A woollen felted cloth, with a heavily napped and raised surface, in imitation of beaver fur. (2) A hat made of this cloth. (3) Expensive genuine beaver skin, also called castor. (4) A kind of cheap leather dyed different colours and used for gloves.

Bedfordshire lace A type of *bobbin- or *bone-lace made in the Bedfordshire area of England.

betilla [betelle, bethille, betille, botilla, bettella] *Muslins or white cotton cloths, woven in Bengal and southern India. There is a great variety in the spelling, as the word had no fixed form.

blonde [blond, blonde lace, blonde net] Figured silk net lace, the creamy colour of raw silk, made by machine and proliferating in fashion after 1808. A source of that year pointed out that 'this silk [is] of a very inferior kind, and not equal to the [linen] thread used in manufacturing the other laces, [and] will not permit the blond to be bleached, a process on which depends its chief beauty. Hence the blond lace is not only infinitely less durable, but is also of less value than the ordinary laces.'[33]

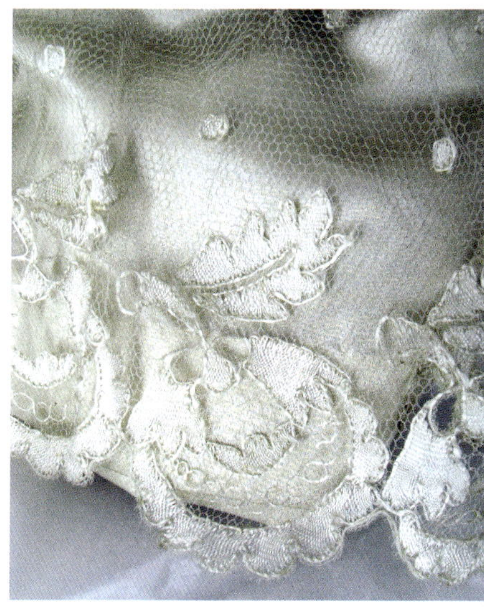

Cuff of blonde lace, c.1815

bobbin-lace Any lace handmade on a lace pillow or cushion using bobbins. Previously called *bone-lace, sometimes called 'pillow' or 'cushion' lace (*cf.* *bobbin net, *patent net, *point net).

bobbin net [bobbinet, bobbinette, British net] A machine-made lace, imitating fine *bobbin- or 'pillow' lace, plain-woven in a hexagonal mesh of four sides twisted and two crossed over; it was usually made of silk and cotton. *Tulle is a kind of bobbin net. John Heathcoat's second bobbin net machine of 1809 finally perfected this machine-made net, and reproduced exactly the twisting action of handmade lace, instead of the looping of *point net machines. From 1815, bobbin net manufacture superseded that of point net and *patent net.

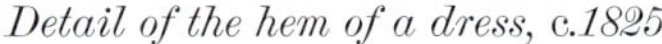

Detail of the hem of a dress, c.1825

bombazet [bombazett, bombazette] A twilled fabric of cotton and *worsted, or of worsted alone, cheaper than *bombazine. It was used for *mourning, and for coloured day gowns.

bombazine [bombasin, bombasine, bombazin, bombazeen] A twilled fabric made of silk alone, of silk and *worsted, of cotton with silk, or of worsted alone; it was often black, and in this colour was used for *mourning dress. The name derives from *Bombyx*, the genus of silk moths.

Bombazine with red silk warp and coarser brown wool weft, 1770s

bone-lace A linen and then cotton lace first made in France and Flanders, and thereafter in England, using bone or ivory bobbins instead of wooden ones. The name distinguished the product from *point or needle lace, and was superseded by *bobbin lace.

book muslin [bouk, buke] A plain-weave, very light, transparent *muslin, originally shipped from India in a 'book-fold' bale. It was the lightest quality of muslin available, coming after *mull.

British muslin Any *muslin produced in Lancashire, Scotland, or other British textile manufactories.

broadcloth A plain- or *twill-woven fabric of fine woollen yarn, highly *fulled, sometimes with a slightly lustrous finish; it was used in men's coats and suits. Traditionally broadcloth was two yards wide rather than one, though the term came to denote quality rather than width, which varies. In this period, it was 45 to 54 inches (114–137 cm) wide.

brocade A textile fabric, usually silk, richly wrought or 'flowered' with a raised pattern. Brocading was ornamental, not part of the fabric's structure, created with a supplementary weft during weaving that created distinctive floating threads on the textile's reverse. Brocaded sections on textiles can be mistaken for embroidery.

Brussels lace [Brussels point] Fine-quality, expensive, handmade *bobbin or needlepoint lace, or sometimes these techniques combined, usually with a fine hexagonal mesh and floral patterns outlined by a woven edging; it was made in Brussels and the vicinity, and was considered the highest-quality lace.

Linen Brussels appliqué lace border, c.1800–15

Buckinghamshire lace A type of *bobbin- or *bone-lace made in the Buckinghamshire area of England.

buckram Loosely woven coarse fabric made from cotton, hemp or flax stiffened with gum, calendered (polished) and used for lining hats, coats, etc. Buckram was commonly made from old sheets and pieces of old sails, rather than using new cloth for the purpose.

buckskin A creamy white or yellowish leather made from the skin of a male fallow deer, popular for riding *breeches and *gloves.

Buckskin breeches, 1800–25

buff [buff-skin, buff-leather] A kind of thick, dull, yellowish-beige-coloured leather originally made from buffalo skin, but also tanned from elks, oxen and similar animals.

bugle A straight, tubular glass bead, or decoration with such beads.

button Buttons came in every shape, size and material, depending on their purposes as fastenings or decoration. Some were made of gold and silver lace, or of wooden moulds covered in yarns including *mohair, silk, *horsehair and *thread, or covered with fabric, or with *twist silk needle-woven into decorative patterns, called twist buttons. Men's legwear usually had two- or four-hole bone, horn, mother of pearl, glass or metal buttons, or flat metal, lacquer or self-fabric buttons covered with a shank for their functional closures. Men's *coats tended to have flat or domed brass, gilt, cut-steel, pressed, or other metal or covered buttons with a shank for everyday wear. Gilt buttons could have raised insignia. For male decorative *dress buttons, see *buttons (J). Underwear and women's light dresses used thread or *Singleton buttons. *Shirts (M) used thread, glass or bone buttons.

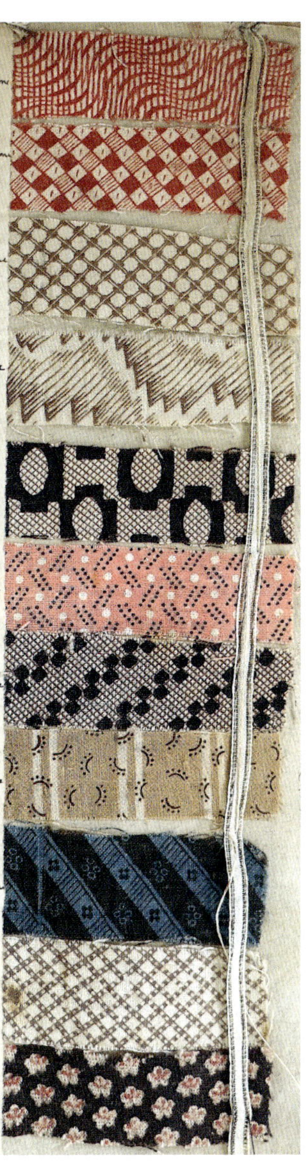

calico [calico] Originally a plain-weave cotton cloth, imported from India in many grades, taking its name from the Keralan city of Calicut (Kozhikode), and usually printed or painted; the term soon came to mean any cotton imported from the East and, eventually, any cotton fabric, including those of European manufacture, and those with warps of other fibres such as linen. Printed calico could be washed without the design's colour bleeding. Calico was used in *morning and day dress, and for other informal or domestic clothing. (Unbleached calico is now called 'muslin' in American English, and 'calico' means any of various cheap cotton fabrics with figured patterns.)

Textile samples of calicoes, late 18th century

calimanco [callimanco, calamanco] A highly glazed, plain or twilled woollen or *worsted cloth, plain, striped, checked, watered or figured; it was popular for waistcoats.

Textile samples of calimancos, late 18th century

cambric [French lawn] A fine linen or hard-spun cotton fabric, originally from Cambrai in France, and either white or dyed and printed. When imported into Britain, it was known as French lawn. The surface was often rolled or calendered to achieve a

slight lustre. Linen cambrics' cost and fine quality were in part originally created by cutting the flax plants before they were fully grown, when the fibres were softer and finer. 'Long lawn' made from flax in Ireland, and Scottish cotton cambrics, were a competitive substitute for the expensive and heavily regulated French original. Colourful British-made printed cotton cambrics were popular for domestic *undress gowns.

Cambric muslin sample from making a gown, 1814

cambric muslin A cotton fabric more densely woven and less transparent than *muslin, made in imitation of linen *cambric fabric; it was popular for women's *morning and day dress, and for small accessories. Cambric muslin could also refer to a somewhat coarser cloth, likewise finished with a glaze, often used for linings of garments and headwear.

camlet [camblet, camlette, chamblet] A hard-wearing fabric woven from mixed threads of wool, especially camel or goat, and silk. In some camlets, the warp was made of wool and silk, and the weft of hair. Camlets could be figured, watered and waved.

Canterbury muslin A coloured *muslin woven from cotton and silk, invented by master weaver John Callaway of Canterbury *c.*1779 to give work to silk weavers when silk imports were scarce due to the American Revolutionary War (1775–83), and manufactured thereafter.

carmelite A fine, soft, plain-woven woollen or *worsted cloth, generally of a dark colour, used for women's outer garments.

cartisane A small piece of thin cardboard, parchment or vellum, around which thread, silk, gold or silver has been wrapped to form an applied embellishment for a gown.

Hem of an evening dress, cartisanes on silk net, c.1820

cashmere The soft hair of the cashmere goat (*Capra aegagrus hircus*), and the light, warm and soft woollen cloth made from it.

cassimere [casimir, cassimer, casimer, cassimire] *See* *kerseymere.

castor *See* *beaver.

castorine *See* *vicuna.

catgut (1) A linen canvas for embroidery. (2) Coarse corded cloth used for linings. (3) A kind of lace.

chambray [chambery, chamberry] A type of *changeable weave where the warp and weft are made of two different colours, often with a coloured warp and a white filling, from the same linguistic origin as *cambric, as a variant of *cambrai*. Chambray could be made from any fibre combination, including silk, cotton, silk and wool, or silk and cotton. Hence Chambray muslin or Chambray gauze.

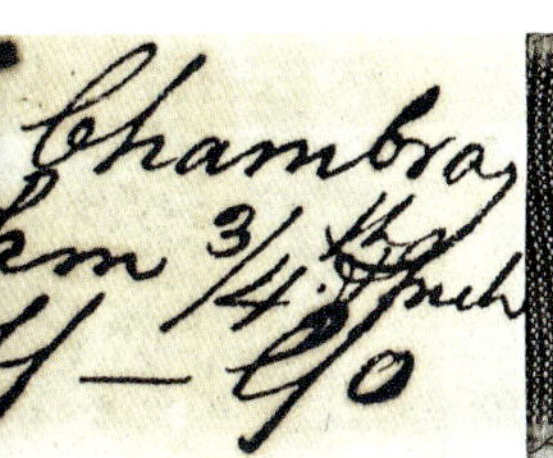

Textile sample of chambray, 1800–25

chamois [chamois-leather, shammy, shamois, shamois-leather, shamoy, shammoy] A leather originally prepared from the skin of the chamois goat, then referring to a soft, pliable, buff-coloured leather prepared from the skins of sheep, goats, deer, calves, and the split hides of other animals. Particularly used to make fine, soft gloves.

changeable Any textile, usually silk, woven with different colours in its warp and weft, like the modern 'shot'. *See also* *mistake ribbon.

chenille [shenneel] (Fr. 'caterpillar') Soft, fluffy silk embroidery thread.

chicken-skin A very thin, flexible, bright yellow suede leather, made from the hides of unborn calves, kids or lambs; it was used for gloves, especially *Limerick gloves (F).

China crape [Canton crape, crepe] Made of fine silk with more threads in the warp than the weft, and a high twist in the yarn which creates a springy, soft body to the fabric, and a matte surface. It was usually used for *gowns worn in the evening, to dinners, balls or the opera, and is distinct from the semi-transparent, crinkled mourning *crape. Now called crêpe de Chine.

Dress of damasked cream china crape (detail), c.1818–20

chiné (Fr.) *See* *cloud.

chintz A fabric of cotton, linen or combination-fibre *calico, fast-printed or hand-painted in numerous colours with floral and other patterns, and usually glazed; it was imported from India. From Hindi, via the Sanskrit word *chitra*, meaning 'variegated'.

'A sprigged chintz, designed for morning dresses', September 1811

chip (1) Very long thin pliable strips of willow or other wood, plaited together to make material for *hats; it was usually painted or dyed black or white, but is occasionally seen in fashion plates in green, blue, yellow and other colours. (2) Hats made from the leaves of the Cuban palm, plaited.

A woven chip or willow bonnet with a cawl, trim and lining of striped brown cotton, c.1805–10

chord Alternative spelling of *cord.

cloth Properly, any fabric made from wool woven on a loom, which is how the word is usually used in the Regency period.

cloud [clouded, *chiné*] A silk, cotton or mixed textile where the pattern or stripe has been dyed in the yarn before weaving. Pre-

dyeing threads produces a soft and blurred 'cloudy' effect in the pattern, most familiar in the Southeast Asian textile technique of *ikat*. Any type of weave could be a cloud, as in a clouded satin, for example. In silk it was better known as *chiné*, after the French manufacture inspired by silks originally woven in China.

Textile pattern sample of a clouded silk (detail), 1792

coating Thick, heavy wool cloth used for making *coats.

cord [Bedford cord, patent cord] Sturdy wool, *worsted, or cotton and wool fabric, woven with a raised cord or ridge running in the warp.

cording (1) Fine cotton *cord covered with fabric, applied to a garment for decoration and to reinforce seams; it is now called 'piping'. (2) Very narrow *rouleaux with the appearance of covered cord.

Detail of a figured silk pelisse cuff with rouleaux and cording, c.*1820*

corduroy [corderoy] A sturdy, hard-wearing cotton fabric, with thick ridges or cords of short, velvety pile; it was used for breeches, waistcoats and coats, especially for rural and working dress. It was a type of fustian; *see* *fustian (2).

Sample card of corduroys, late eighteenth century

cotton The soft and downy fibre growing around seeds of the cotton plant (genus *Gossypium*). Fabrics made from cotton were the most influential and transformative during the Regency period. Indian cottons had been imported for centuries, and were valued for their lightness, colour-fastness and washability. Competing with and imitating these popular textiles to a high quality was a major impetus for Britain's industrialised textile production, although manufacturers' supplies relied heavily on enslaved labour on cotton plantations in the United States and Caribbean. From pure cotton fabrics such as *chintz and *calico being used primarily for outer garments in the late eighteenth century, the fibre became increasingly present in details of clothing such as *linings, *cording and tapes; or used for *stockings and undergarments, slowly replacing the traditional linen, although some people complained that cotton was less durable during laundering, and did not wear as well as linen. For textiles and trimmings wholly or partly made with cotton fibres, *see* *alepine, *betilla, *bobbin net, *bombazet, *bombazine, *bone-lace, *buckram, *calico, *cambric, *cambric muslin, *Canterbury muslin, *chambray, *chintz, *cloud, *cord, *corduroy, *coutil, *dimity, *dowlas, *ferret, *fleecy-hosiery, *fustian, *gauze, *gimp, *gingham, *gurrah, *jaconet, *japan, *jean, *jeanet, *kersey, lace, *lawn, *leno, *Madras check, *marcella, *mohair, *moleskin, *muslin, *nainsook, *nankeen, *percale, *pique, *sateen, *seersucker, *shirting, *stockinette, *swansdown (2), *swanskin, *velveret.

coutil (Fr. 'ticking', 'drill') A strong, close-textured linen (and, later, cotton) fabric, woven in herringbone twill. The word was used increasingly in English from the Regency period.

crape A light semi-transparent fabric, woven from wool or gummed silk, in a plain weave with a distinctive dull, crinkled surface achieved by extreme twisting of the fibres. Black crape was widely used for *mourning dress, partly because of its non-reflective quality. *See also* *China crape, which was opaque, and *Norwich crape.

Wedding dress of crape and satin (detail), 1812

crewel [cruel] Coloured embroidery yarn made of fine, loosely twisted two-ply *worsted. Hence 'crewel-work' for embroidery done with this yarn.

cyprus [cyprus gauze] A fine, light linen.

damask A fabric made of any fibre with reversible patterns woven into it using two contrasting faces (sides) of a weave, often *twill or the different sides of *satin weave, one glossy (warp-float) and one dull (weft-float). The same pattern appears in the opposite weave combination on the back.

dimity A stout white cotton, plain or twilled, with fine ribs or woven-in decoration on one side; it might be plain or printed with a pattern in one or more colours. It was popular for *morning dress, waistcoats, and accessories such as detachable pockets.

A white dimity cotton waistcoat printed with fine blue stripes, c.1800–10

Dorset button Any of several types of *thread button, made of metal rings wrapped with thread in decorative patterns.

dowlas [dowl] A heavy, coarse linen or cotton fabric, used for shirts and smocks.

drab A thick, closely woven woollen cloth, of a yellowish, grey or brown colour, often used in *great coats, sometimes double-milled (see *fulling); also, these colours in any context.

drill A sturdy, twilled linen fabric, popular for men's trousers, breeches and lightweight upper garments; *see also* *coutil.

drugget (1) A double-milled *baize. (2) Any heavy woollen fabric sufficiently coarse, with a warp and weft of different fibres, usually linen, silk, wool or *worsted. If twill-woven, known as a corded drugget.

duck Strong, plain-woven white or natural linen fabric, often with double warp and double weft threads; it was frequently used for trousers and summer coats.

duffel [duffield, duffil] A coarse woollen fabric with a thick nap on both sides; also an overcoat made of this fabric. It was named for the Belgian town of Duffel.

elastic A description of any textile with a springy stretch in it, usually knitted. Elastic materials with rubber in them to increase the stretch, like modern elastic, were patented by Thomas Hancock on 29 April 1820: 'For an improvement in the application of a certain material to various articles of dress', including the wrists of gloves, waistcoat backs and waist-bands, pockets, *trouser and *gaiter straps, *braces, *stockings, *garters and *stays, and 'to boots, shoes, clogs and pattens, when the object is to put them on and off without lacing or tying'.[34]

ermine The pure white winter fur of the European stoat or short-tailed weasel (*Mustela erminea*). It is represented in images the way it was fashioned, with the black tail tip added as spotted contrast to the white.

everlasting [lasting] A stout, closely double-*twill-woven *worsted *stuff.

eyelet [oilet, oilet hole] A hole for decoration, or to pass a cord or *string through, made by sewing with thread around the hole in a circle to reinforce it. Metal eyelets were not invented until 1828.

feather Feathers in use in Regency fashion included bird of paradise, grebe, marabou [marabouts, maraboo], ostrich, paroquet [parrot], partridge, peacock and swansdown (not to be confused with the textile *swansdown [T]).

ferret [ferrett, ferrit, ferritt] A narrow, strong binding tape of silk, wool or cotton, often used for binding and tying.

festoon Puffs of material decorating the seams and/or edges of a woman's garment.

figured A textile that is patterned or otherwise ornamented, usually by having the design woven in.

Alfred Edward Chalon, Princess Charlotte of Wales, Princess of Saxe-Coburg-Saalfeld, *with an ermine-trimmed coat and muff*, c.1817–19

flannel A somewhat loosely woven plain-weave or twilled cloth of undyed (cream) woollen yarn, of variable fineness, with a fluffy, raised nap on at least one side. Historically, it was called 'Welsh cotton' after its traditional place of manufacture. Later manufactures could include a cotton warp. It was soft, washable, warm, light and comfortable, and therefore used extensively for men's and women's undergarments, including *shirts, *waistcoats, *drawers, *jumps and *petticoats, as well as for *dressing and other soft wrapping gowns. Not to be confused with the modern 'flannel', which is an abbreviation for the cotton 'flannelette' later nineteenth-century manufacturers made to imitate the wool original.

Admiral Lord Nelson's flannel waistcoat, c.1800

fleecy-hosiery A fleecy knitted wool or cotton fabric interwoven with fine parts of wool on one side, looking like hosiery on one side and fleecy wool on the other, used to make stockings, socks, waistcoats and other warm clothing, and for making false calves in stockings to enhance the wearer's shape.

florentine [florentine satin, florentine silk] (1) A twilled or satin silk fabric, made striped, figured or plain, often used in men's evening *waistcoats and *breeches. (2) A *worsted *stuff.

floss [silk floss] (1) The rough, short fibres shed in the winding of silk cocoons; these fibres were carded and made into common silk fabrics. (2) The long silk fibres used, untwisted, in embroidery.

French lawn *See* *cambric. *Linon* in French.

French wadding *See* *wadding.

frieze A coarse, warm woollen cloth with a rough, twisted nap. Friezing or frizing (like frizzing hair) was the process of twisting hairs of the cloth's raised pile into each other, by hand or mechanically, to form little raised naps, or burls, thickly and evenly spread over the surface of the cloth. Used for outer garments. Friezes could not be made of wholly *worsted cloths, as they have no pile to twist.

fulling A finishing process for woollen cloth that felts, compresses and thickens the fibres through scouring and pressing, raising the nap and obscuring the weave; the finished cloth is described as 'fulled' or milled. Double-milled cloth was fulled twice.

fur The skin of an animal tanned with the hair left on, prized for the quality of the hair. Animal furs in use for clothing, accessories and garment trimming during the Regency period included: Astrakhan [Astracan], bear, chinchilla [chinchealley, chingchelli], *ermine, fox, hare, *lambskin, leopard, lynx, marten [pine marten], miniver (fur from the belly of a squirrel), mink, mole, nutria (musk beaver or coypu), otter [sea-otter], rabbit [coney], raccoon, sable, seal [seal-skin], squirrel and wolf.

Sir Thomas Lawrence, John Arthur Douglas Bloomfield, 2nd Baron Bloomfield, *1819*

furbelow [falbela] A flounce or ruffle on a woman's *petticoat, scarf, apron or sometimes *gown; it was usually made of the same fabric as the item it adorned, or of lace.

fustian (1) Originally, a coarse, twilled fabric of linen warp and cotton weft, but later any textile made of mixed linen or hemp and cotton, or any coarse cotton cloth. Fustians could be wide, narrow or coarse, with shag or nap, and without. (2) During the Regency, a thick, twilled, grey-brown cotton, with a short, velvety nap, like *corduroy, but without ribs; it was used in rural and working dress.

Detail of cotton fustian breeches, 1800–15

galloon [gallon] Narrow, close-woven *ribbon or braid, made of wool, thread, gold, silver, mohair or silk, used as trimming for *hats, *capes and other items of clothing.

gauging [gaging] Gathers made and fixed with thread, as in smocking, rather than drawn up on a cord or tape.

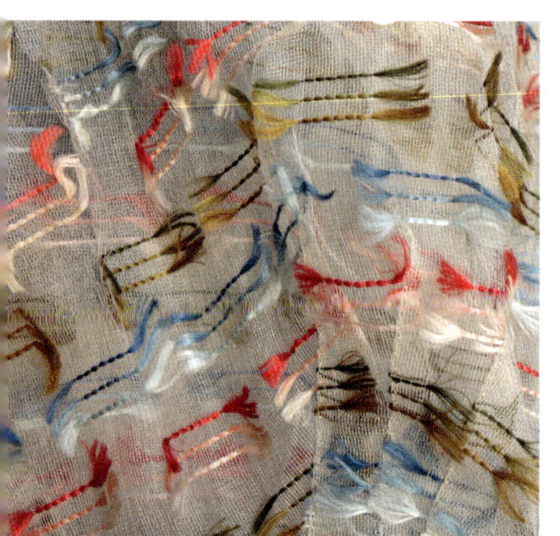

gauze [gause, gaze] A fine, thin, transparent, open-weave fabric, usually made of silk, but sometimes of linen or cotton; the dual warp threads are twisted around the weft to give firmness. It was popular for women's *evening dress.

Detail of the bodice of an evening dress made of silk gauze woven with silk floss tufts, 1810s

gimp [gymp] An openwork trimming or braid, made by twisting silk, cotton or *worsted yarns around wire or cord to create a sturdy texture, then plaiting or braiding the resulting threads together. From French, *guimpe*.

gingham A firm, medium-weight linen or (more often) cotton cloth; the yarn was dyed and woven in checks or stripes, and the fabric was sometimes glazed like chintz. Often 32 inches (81 cm) wide. Gingham originally came from India.

glazing A finishing process for textiles in which a glossy substance is applied to the fabric which is then calendered, usually with rollers, to achieve a smooth, glossy surface; such cloth is described as 'glazed'. *See* image for *calimanco (p. 187).

gold muslin Any *muslin embroidered with gold or gilt threads.

Hem of a muslin round gown embroidered and fringed with gilt metal, c.1795

grogram A coarse *taffeta, of silk and wool or *mohair, woven diagonally. The English name for the French *grosgrain.

gros de Naples [gros-de-Naples, gro de nap] A plain-weave silk with a slight corded or ribbed effect created by having the weft yarns thicker than the warp yarns, originally made in Naples, Italy, similar to *lutestring, lighter than *gros de Tours and stronger than *taffeta, often with two different colours in the warp and weft. Both gros de Naples and gros de Tours could be plain, striped, embroidered, *figured or woven with metallic threads.

gros de Tours [gros de tours, gros-de-Tours, gros-de-tours] A plain-weave thick silk with a corded or ribbed effect created by having the weft yarns thicker than the warp yarns, first made in Tours, France, as an imitation of *gros de Naples, then produced in other places. It differed from gros de Naples in having two warp yarns pass over or under the weft yarn at each row, instead of one in the lighter fabric.

Weaver's sample of silk gros de Tours, c.1816

grosgrain (Fr.) *See* *grogram.

gum flowers *Artificial flowers made from *cambric or silk, stiffened with gum arabic and dried on glass; the use of gum resulted in a smooth, glossy finish.

gurrah Coarse, thick, plain cotton cloth made in northeastern India; it was often printed after importation to European countries.

Hanover lace The meaning of this term is uncertain. It may refer to a variation of *Honiton lace, a *bobbin-lace like *Brussels lace but coarser, and with simpler applied patterns. The use of the term in the context of poor work suggests a base of machine-made *net with decorations of small, embroidered flowers.

hard tartan Tartan cloth woven from *worsted yarn.

Holland Originally, linen fabric imported from Holland, though the name became generic for many linens. When unbleached, it was called 'brown Holland'. Holland was frequently used to line coats and other outer garments, but it was also used for shirts and gowns.

Honiton lace An expensive handmade lace made in the vicinity of Honiton in Devonshire, resembling *Brussels lace with the floral or *sprig decorations made separately and sewn on afterwards.

Border made of Honiton lace appliqué on machine-made net ground, early 19th century

hook and eye A two-part fastening used to close male and female jackets, coats and dresses. The metal hook, usually made from brass, could pass into a corresponding metal loop or eye, or a worked *eyelet hole. On many back-fastening *gowns the *buttons were ornamental, and hooks and eyes underneath were actually keeping the bodice closed.

horsehair [horse hair, horse-hair] Thick, strong hairs from the tails of horses woven into an equally durable fabric. When plaited together, it was used to make *hats, *bonnets, belts and *bracelets.

hunter A strong, thick double-milled (see *fulling) woollen *kersey fabric, used for *top coats and *great coats.

Irish [Irish linen] Plain-weave Irish linen, used for nightwear, undergarments and many miscellaneous accessories. It 'constitutes one of the most useful and necessary parts of an Englishman's dress',[35] and was widely used. The $\frac{7}{8}$ (80 cm) and 1 yard (91 cm) widths came in 'pieces' of about 18–25 yards long (16.5–22.9 m), and the $1\frac{1}{8}$ (102 cm), $1\frac{1}{4}$ (114 cm) and $1\frac{1}{2}$ yards (137 cm) width came in much longer pieces of 60–75 yards (54.9–68.6 m).

Italian straw Any straw used for hats imported from Italy. *See* *Leghorn for an explanation of the quality.

jaconet [jacconet, jacconot, jackonet, jaconet muslin, jaconot] A thin plain-weave cotton, of a weight between *muslin and *cambric; it was popular for women's *morning dress. Although the word sounds French, it was of Indian origin, which accounts for some of the varieties in spelling. It could be woven with stripes or cording running through it.

'A striped Scotch jaconet muslin', September 1812

japan [japan muslin] A kind of *muslin with a pattern woven in, or 'loom-figured'; 'fancy'; could be *brocaded. Hence also a textile description, as in 'japanned muslin'. Possibly derived from Bengali *jamdani* muslins.

'Japan betilla muslin', May 1815

jean [jane] (1) A stout, twilled cotton fabric, and (in the nineteenth century) also a twilled *sateen. (2) A type of coarse twilled fabric of linen and cotton, used for a wide range of men's and women's clothing, especially *trousers, *stays, *corsets and *shoes, and for *linings (*see also* *fustian [1]).

jeanet A slightly lighter type of *jean.

joining lace Any narrow lace woven with straight edges each side, used as a decorative join when 'let-in' to fabrics, especially on gowns. Sometimes called 'letting-in' lace.

Detail of a muslin gown with handmade joining lace inserts, c.*1810*

kersey A stout, somewhat coarse double-twilled fabric made of wool, or of wool with a cotton warp, closely napped, and heavier than *broadcloth. It was effective for repelling cold and damp, and was used in suits, coats and outerwear, especially by the army and navy, and labouring people. A 1799 dictionary described kersey as being between a *stuff and a *cloth in weight. It was made from the coarsest English wool breeds after the long-staple *worsted fibres were removed. It often came in white, or was dyed *drab, brown, blue and other dark colours.

kerseymere [cassimer, cassimere, casimir, kersimere] An expensive, softer, lighter version of the long-established woollen fabric *kersey, densely 2/2 twill-woven from very fine yarns, preferably Spanish *merino, not given a nap (a raised and cut surface finish obscuring the weave), around 27 inches (68.5 cm)

wide. Kerseymere was a summer cloth with the warmth and strength of the wider *broadcloth but with less weight. Francis Yerbury of Bradford patented kerseymere in 1766 as 'cassimere', the name sounding like the 'cashmere' fabric made from goats which this sheep's wool product resembled.

'A chintz kerseymere for gentlemen's waistcoats', November 1809

kid A very soft, finely grained, thin pliable leather made from the skins of kids or lambs. Largely used for women's *gloves, and for *shoes. Often imported from France, Spain and Italy, and finished in Britain.

lace (1) Any kind of metallic braid, especially those used on military and naval uniforms. (2) A decorative openwork textile created by twisting, netting or plaiting linen, cotton or silk threads together, by hand using bobbins or by machine. The connection between the two terms is the plaiting actions used in their manufacture. 'Lace' handmade using bobbins worked on a lace cushion to create the whole pattern was technically distinguished from 'point', worked with a needle to create the lace, or to embellish a net ground, such as *Alençon point. *See* *Bedfordshire lace, *blonde, *bobbin net, *bone-lace, *Brussels lace, *catgut, *Hanover lace, *Honiton lace, *joining lace, *Levers lace, *Mechlin lace, *patent net, *Pusher lace, *tinsel.

lama A cloth made from the wool of the llama (*Lama glama*). Not to be confused with the alternative spelling of the fabric *lamé.

lambskin [lamb skin] (1) A fine, pliant leather made from the skin of lambs, used for *gloves, *breeches and *shoes. (2) The same with the wool left attached; a kind of *fur.

lamé [lama, lame, lammy] Light silk *gauze, woven through with silver or gilt threads to create a shimmering metallic surface; it was popular for women's *court and *evening dress.

Detail of the hem of a silk net dress embroidered with lamé, c.1820

lasting *See* *everlasting.

lawn A very fine, quite crisp, somewhat transparent plain-weave linen or later cotton, originally from Laon, France; it was widely used for undergarments, *shirts, *shifts, and any other accessory that could be made of linen or cotton. Lawns could be printed or woven with other colours. For French lawn, *see* *cambric, although lawn is technically woven with finer thread than cambric.

leather The tanned or alum-finished skin of an animal, used for *breeches, *shoes, *boots, *gloves, belts, and other accessories. Coloured leathers were particularly used for women's shoes and gloves. See also *beaver, *buckskin, *buff, *chamois, *chicken-skin, *lambskin, *morocco, *Spanish leather, *swanskin, *wash-leather.

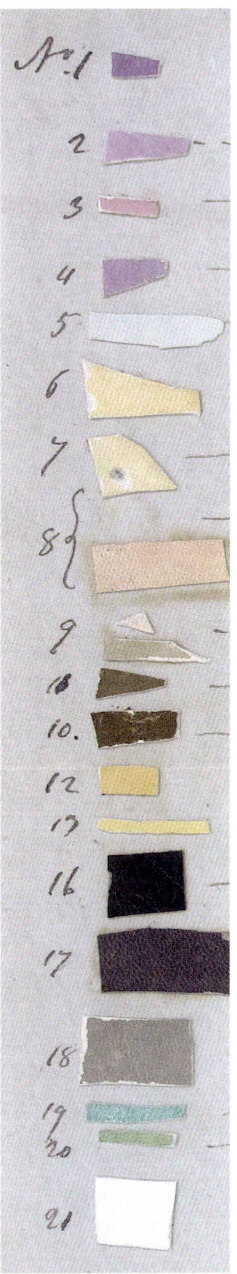

A merchant's sample card of coloured fine leathers, early 19th century

Leghorn [Leghorn chip] A fine, very pliable wheat straw from the Livorno region of Italy, plaited into strips to be made into *headwear; also a *hat or *bonnet made from this straw. Many attempts were made in Britain to imitate the straw's fineness, including using what was then called ticklematch or ticklemoth grass, now tickle grass (*Agrostis scabra*), and couch or spear grass (*Agrostis capillaris*). A newspaper article of 1823 explains the difference in quality between Italian and English straws: 'the importation of the straw hats and bonnets from *Italy*, greatly superior, in durability and beauty, to those made in England. The plat [*sic*] made in England was made of the straw of *ripened grass*. It was, in general, *split*, . . . the Italian plat was made of the straw of grain, or grass, *cut green*. Now, the straw of ripened grass is brittle; or rather, rotten. . . . But besides the difference in point of toughness, strength and durability, there was the difference in beauty. The colour of the Italian plat was better; the plat was brighter, and the Italian straws being *small whole* straws, instead of small straws made by the splitting of large ones, there was a roundness to them, that gave *light and shade* to the plat, which could not be given by our flat bits of straw' (original italics).[36] The straw was also grown smaller, shorter and finer than English straw. When a

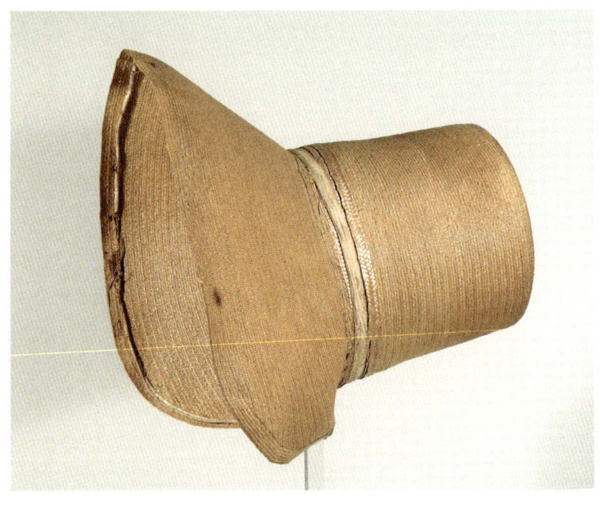

Leghorn straw bonnet, wired brim, cream ribbon band tied in a bow at the right, 1815–20

Leghorn *plait (T) was spiralled around to create headwear, its pliability also meant it could be sewn or looped together edge-to-edge, whereas English plait needed to overlap and be sewn down. Leghorn articles therefore had a smooth, even surface, and English ones were ridged, and consumed more straw.

leno [lino, linau] A type of weave, with the double warp threads being twisted around the weft yarns, creating a durability that offsets its open-weave appearance. Leno was applied as a name to light but strong cotton or linen gauzes woven this way, most often used for caps and veils but sometimes for trimmings and gowns. Lenos could have further decoration applied to them, such as spots, stripes or figures.

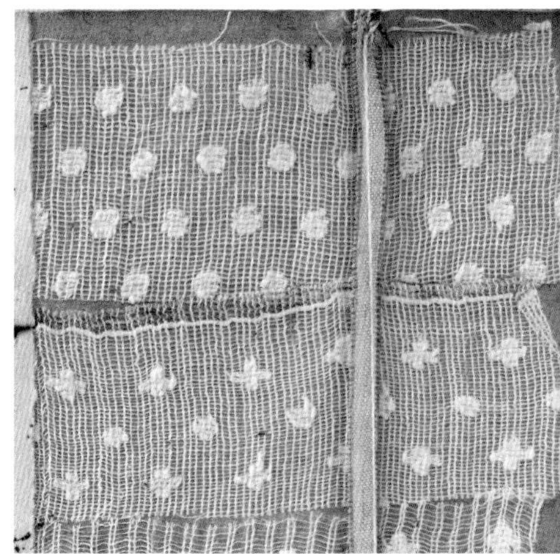

Textile sample of spotted cotton leno, 1800–25

letting-in lace *See* *joining lace.

Levantine A stout, soft, closely woven and 'rich-faced' twilled silk, with good wear. Its front and back sides showed different shades of the weaving threads; if the front was blue-black, the back was jet-black, and vice versa.

Levers lace A kind of *net made on the Levers machine (invented 1813), using Jacquard loom technology (1805) to form patterns, especially zig-zags and V-shapes, and to imitate handmade lace.

linen Fabric made from the processed stems of flax or hemp plants, used especially for undergarments touching the body due to its absorbency and strength, which allows it to endure much tougher laundry treatments. For specific textiles made from linen, *see* *batiste, *cambric, *cambric muslin, *chambray, *coutil,

*cyprus, *damask, *Dorset button, *dowlas, *drill, *duck, *fustian, *gauze, *gingham, *Holland, *Irish, *jean, *lawn, *leno, *linsey-wolsey, *marcella, *thread, *thread buttons, and most varieties of lace.

linsey-wolsey [linsey-woolsey] A coarse fabric of linen warp and wool weft.

list (1) The cut-off selvedges of woollen textiles. (2) A fabric made from weaving the selvedges together, used for *list shoes.

Black wool list boot with leather sole, European, 19th century

love A thin silk, used in black for *mourning wear, or made as *ribbons.

lustre A glossy fabric, woven from silk and worsted, used for women's gowns, especially *evening dress.

*'A bright geraneum [*sic*] lustre for evening wear', February 1812*

lutestring [lustring] A glossy, crisp, plain-weave silk, which could be plain, striped, *changeable, *figured or *brocaded. Not to be confused with *lustre, which has a worsted component.

Madras check [Madras] A firm cotton fabric, woven with checks of varying proportions in dual or multiple colours that were not colour-fast; it was imported from Madras in India, and used in gowns and some accessories.

marcella [marseilles, Marseilles quilting, quilting] A *twill cotton or linen fabric with diaper patterns woven in relief; it was used for smaller dress accessories, especially waistcoats and detachable pockets.

Printed diamond marcella quilting for men's waistcoats, 1809

Mechlin [Mecklin] lace Expensive handmade *bobbin-lace with the pattern outlined in flat thread on a net ground. Originating in Mechelen in the Low Countries, it began to be made by machine in 1819. The handmade variety was the second-highest quality after *Brussels lace.

Melton A thick, well-fulled woollen fabric with a smooth, close nap, normally with a *twill weave; it was popular for *riding-habits and *hunting coats.

merino A fine, warm cloth made from the fleece of the Spanish merino sheep, the equivalent of English *superfine; it was used in women's dress and some tailored garments. Merino was also used to make a very thin *crape.

metal thread embroidery *See* *gold muslin, *silver muslin.

milling [milled] *See* *fulling.

mistake ribbon [mistake ribband] A shot or *changeable silk *ribbon.

Linen Mechlin lace border, early 19th century

mode *See* *alamode.

mohair (1) A soft yarn made from the hair of the Angora goat, and the fabric made from it with a silk, wool or cotton warp. (2) Slang for a non-military civilian man, a bourgeois, tradesman or other worker who wore mohair *buttons, used as a term of contempt by army men, who wore metal buttons on their uniforms.

moiré French for 'watered', used as a description for textiles, often silk, which had permanent water-like patterns created on their surface by passing the cloth over a hot brass cylinder, engraved with patterns, and pressing it between two wooden rollers. The effect often resembled *damask, without the designs being woven in. *See also* *moreen.

moleskin A stout, cotton *fustian, with a fine nap that was cut short before dyeing to give an even, dense texture similar to a mole's fur. It was popular for breeches, trousers and waistcoats, especially for men's sporting and labouring dress. Versions could be made in silk with a longer pile for women's dress, similar to a *shag. For the skins of moles, see fur.

moreen [morain] A name probably derived from **moiré*. A kind of *camlet.

morocco [morocco leather] A thin, fine, supple leather traditionally prepared from goatskin, but sheep or split calf skins were also used. Used in dress chiefly for *shoes, wallets, and other accessories. Historically produced in North African and Anatolian regions.

mousseline (Fr.) *Muslin, or a dress made of that fabric. In France, *mousseline* referred to Indian muslins, and British muslin was called *organdie*.

mull [mull muslin, mulmul, mul-mul, mull-mull] An alternative name for *muslin fabric, now the common name for it in American English. From *mul-mul*, the name for muslin in its original Indian areas of production. Mull was very thin, lighter in weight than *jaconet.

muslin A lightweight, semi-transparent, soft cotton fabric originating in Indian areas, particularly Bengal, of a plain weave, usually white but could be coloured; it often had a pattern, either woven in with a supplementary weft (*jamdani*, *jamdanna*), or applied after weaving through embroidery (*chikan*) or *tambour work, and came in many different weights and finishes. Pattern descriptions in English included 'checked', 'clear' (more transparent), 'coloured' (printed or dyed), 'figured' (patterned), 'flowered' (with a floral pattern), 'printed', 'sprigged' (ornamented with small regular floral or plant motifs), 'spotted' (*do-rukha*), 'stained' (dyed), 'striped', and 'worked' (embroidered); the embroidery could be silk, cotton, silver or gilt metal threads (*see* *gold muslin, *silver muslin). Muslin could be opaque if the threads were densely woven, and differed from *calicoes in fineness of thread, weave and breadth, being 34–6 inches (86–91 cm) wide. Muslin was also manufactured en masse in the British Isles, particularly Scotland, from the 1770s onwards. Muslin

Indian muslin, probably made for the European market, c.1800

was also the term for the type of fine yarn used. Indian muslin threads were spun from varieties of the cotton species *Gossypium herbaceum* with a particularly fine, soft fibre, and handwoven into textiles. British muslins used American cotton fibres, spun by machine and woven on hand- or power-looms, which increased the production speed. It was said that: 'British muslins acquire a yellowish cast, after they have been repeatedly washed, while the genuine India-muslins retain their original whiteness.'[37] *See also* *betilla, *book muslin, *calico, *cambric muslin, *Canterbury muslin, *jaconet, *japan, *mousseline, *mull, *nainsook, *organdie.

nainsook [nansouk, nansook] A soft, fine kind of *muslin, often striped. The name came from Hindi *nainsukh*, meaning 'eyes' delight'.

nankeen [nankin, nanqueen, nanquin] A fabric made from a naturally yellowish-brown or tan-coloured variety of cotton (*Gossypium hirsutum*). White nankeen was a cream colour. Originally made in Nanjing (Nankin, Nanking), China, it was popular for men's dress including trousers and waistcoats, and women's shoes and coats. British nankeens were at this time considered of inferior quality to the genuine article.

Nankeen tailcoat, c.1815–20

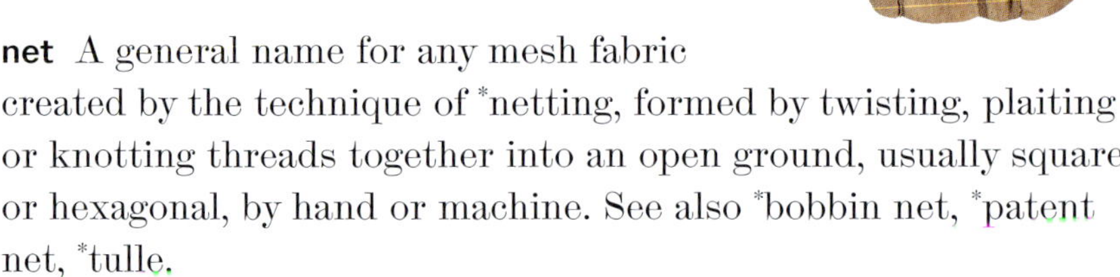

net A general name for any mesh fabric created by the technique of *netting, formed by twisting, plaiting or knotting threads together into an open ground, usually square or hexagonal, by hand or machine. See also *bobbin net, *patent net, *tulle.

netting A technique of looping and knotting thread into an open mesh, done with a netting needle or shuttle, and a netting gauge. Popular for purses and outer dresses.

Netted cotton dress, c.1798

Norwich crape A black, twill, soft woollen textile, distinct from all-silk *crape. After 1819, a modern 'Norwich crape' fabric was invented, plain-woven of fine silk and worsted, with a glossy finish, similar to *bombazine.

Norwich stuff A general term for *worsted and worsted-blend fabrics manufactured in East Anglia.

organdie (Fr.) In France, *mousseline* referred to Indian muslins, and *British and *book muslin was called *organdie*.

osnaburgh [osnaberg, osnabruck, osnabrug, ozenbrig, osnaburg] A kind of strong, coarse, unbleached linen, originally made at Osnabrück in Germany. Similar to *dowlas.

pasteboard Rolled and compressed paper, used for *bonnet *fronts (W).

patent net [patent lace, pattinet, point net] A general term for machine-made lace arising from innovations in lace-making machines from 1778 onwards, when Thomas Taylor patented a point net machine which made lace through looping techniques, using one continuous thread, contrasting with the netting

techniques used in handmade lace. Other improvements in machines during the 1790s made 'patent' or double-press point net of silk popular in fashion. However, silk patent net needed to be stiffened with gum arabic or similar substances to maintain the hexagonal ground appearance. If it got even damp, the textile shrank and crumpled, and, if a thread was cut, it could unravel. Patent or point net could be made of double cotton threads from 1804, but thanks to a market flooded with cheaper single cotton thread, and the invention of *bobbin net, it was rapidly superseded by about 1815.

Silk double point machine-made patent net, detail on a dress, c.1795

percale [perkale] A glazed, fine cotton cloth, similar to *cambric muslin, but less expensive; usually white or blue or printed, it was popular for *morning dress.

Persian A thin, light, soft, plain-woven silk, frequently used to line garments; it was similar to, but lighter and cheaper than, *sarcenet.

Detail of the Persian lining of Jane Austen's pelisse, 1812–14

pique [piqué, piquet, picket] A stiff cotton fabric, woven in a strongly ribbed or raised pattern.

plain As a description of fabric, meaning without any decoration, either woven in or applied.

plain weave The basic structure of weaving, with one thread over and one thread under the other.

plait [plat, platt] (T) A braided strip of *straw or very thin willow (*see* *chip), used in multiples and sewn together to make hats and bonnets.

plush A kind of *velvet with a long, loose pile or *shag, for which fabric it was sometimes a synonym. It was usually woven with a single wool weft and a double warp, one yarn being wool, the other mohair, goat or camel hair, or sometimes silk, then distinguished from velvet by the length of its pile. Some plush was woven wholly from *worsted, and often called *shag. Plush was popular for men's *waistcoats.

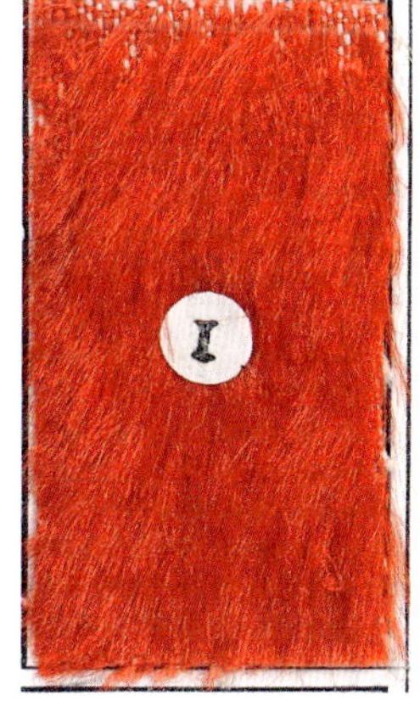

Mohair plush, cheaper than silk plush, January 1809

point lace *See* lace.

point net A general term for lace machine-made through a looping technique, used interchangeably with *patent net in this period.

poplin A lightweight dress fabric with a light *worsted weft and a dense silk warp, which either completely covered the coarser woollen yarns to create a corded or ribbed effect, or was an even plain weave. Poplins differed from *bombazines in having a higher silk proportion, and were very similar to *tabbinets.

Detail of a mustard yellow poplin dress, 1810s

prunella [prunello, prunell] A lightweight, *twill, warp-faced *worsted fabric; it was usually black, and was used so often for clerical garments that the name became a synonym for 'clergyman'. Prunella was also popular for women's footwear.

Pusher lace A kind of openwork lace made on a Pusher machine (invented 1812).

Satin ribbon quilling, trimming a wedding dress hem (detail), 1812

quilling [quiling] A thin strip of fabric or lace, arranged or gathered into box pleats, ripples or folds by means of stitching, and used for decoration, often as an edging.

quilting Another word for *marcella.

rateen A general name in commerce for *drugget, *baize, *frieze, and other coarse, thick wool-based cloths.

ribbon [riband, ribband] A length of narrow, fine fabric, usually of silk, used as edging or decoration on garments, millinery and soft furnishings, as a hair ornament and fastening, or to tether articles together attractively. In England, the penny was the measurement unit for ribbons. As an 1841 encyclopaedia explains, 'Ribbons are made according to a fixed standard of widths designated by different numbers of pence, which once no doubt denoted the price of the article, but at present have reference only to its breadth.'[38] Technically, it was a 'riband', but the common spelling eventually became the usual one.

rouleau [rouleaux [plural], rolio, rollio] Narrow strips of bias-cut fabric, sewn into tubes and applied in decorative patterns to women's clothing.

Detail of rouleaux on the front of a silk pelisse, c.1820

sarcenet [sarsenet, sarsnet] A fine, light fabric made from 'soft' (ungummed) silk, either plain or twilled, with a slight sheen; it was widely used for *linings as well as outer garments, and could be woven with patterns or *figured. Popular for gowns and headwear. It was roughly midway between the crispness of *taffeta and the soft, dull drape of *crape; a thinner, lighter kind of *lutestring.

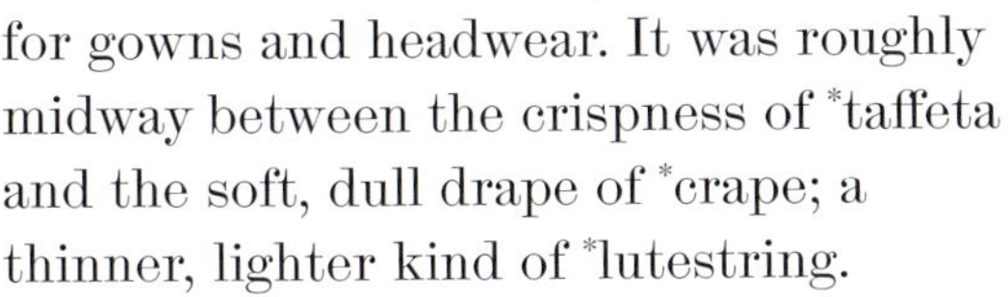

Red and blue silk sarcenet, c.1810

sateen [satteen] Satin-woven cotton cloths, often with the satin-faced warp running horizontally instead of vertically.

satin [sattin] Any fabric constructed by the satin-weave method, one of the three basic textile weaves, usually of silk. The fabric is characterised by a smooth surface and usually a lustrous face and dull back; it is made in a wide variety of weights for various uses, including *dresses, particularly *evening wear, and could be *figured. If woven in cotton it was called *sateen, and in wool or *worsted, *satinet.

satinet *Satin fabric woven from wool or *worsted.

say [saye] A type of woollen *serge fabric (from the Dutch *saai*). Either $\frac{7}{8}$ (80 cm) or $\frac{3}{4}$ (69 cm) of a yard wide.

seersucker A striped fabric of Indian origin, woven of silk and cotton, often with a rippled effect produced by weaving the cotton warps with a looser tension than the silk ones.

serge (1) A hard-wearing, *twill cloth of worsted warp and wool weft, or wholly of worsted, having a smooth face with a slight sheen. It was often sold in undyed white. The twill weave differentiated it from *baize. (2) **[Silk serge]** A twill silk fabric with distinctive diagonal ridge lines, commonly used for the linings of men's *waistcoats and *coats.

shag A *worsted cloth with a long velvet nap on one side; quality ranging from coarse to fine. Sometimes a synonym for *plush.

A wool pelisse with a silk shag imitation fur trim, c.1815–20

shalloon A cheap, double-twilled, *worsted fabric used for lining clothes. It could be unglazed or glazed, like *calimanco.

shirting Any linen or cotton fabric used to make *shirts.

shoe binding A narrow tape of plain-weave silk, used to bind the top edges and cover the outer side seams of *shoes, especially women's, and men's evening *pumps.

silesia [Silesia] A thin, *twill linen cloth, used for *linings, especially those of outer garments.

silk A strong natural protein fibre produced from the cocoons of the larvae of the mulberry silkworm *Bombyx mori*. Its shimmering appearance comes from the fibre reflecting light. The unbroken length of continuous filament unwound from the cocoons also contributes to silk's glossy qualities. The fibre is then formed into yarn or thread, and woven, twisted, netted or knitted into a range of textiles, often with other animal or vegetable fibres. *See* *alamode, *alepine, *atlas, *blonde, *bobbin net, *bombazet, *bombazine, *brocade, *camlet, *Canterbury muslin, *cartisane, *chambray, *changeable, *chenille, *China crape, *cloud, *crape, *drugget, *ferret, *florentine, *floss, *galloon, *gauze, *gimp, *grogram, *gros de Naples, *gum flowers, *lamé, *Levantine, *love, *lustre, *lutestring, **moiré*, *patent net, *Persian, *plush, *poplin, *ribbon, *sarcenet, *satin, *seersucker, *shag, *tabbinet, *taffeta, *tiffany, *tinsel, *tissue, *twist, *velvet, *velveret, *zephyrene.

silver muslin Any *muslin embroidered with silver or silver-gilt threads. The embroidery often appears dark grey or black on historic objects due to tarnishing.

Border from a gown of Indian muslin embroidered with silver lamé, c.1800

Singleton button A flat *button made by covering a wire circle in fabric and sewing through the layers.

An unused card of best-quality Singleton buttons, early 19th century

spangle A small, round, thin piece of glittering metal, including brass, silver gilt or gilt, with a hole in the centre or at the edge to pass a thread through, used for the decoration of textiles. Similar to the modern sequin.

Hem of a white Indian muslin gown, embellished with gilt spangles (detail), c.1805–10

Spanish leather Finely grained leather, of a similar quality to *morocco leather.

sprig Any small flower or plant pattern, embroidered into or printed onto textiles. Hence, 'sprigged'.

stockinette (1) A plain, machine-knitted fabric, its name deriving from 'stocking stitch'. (2) A twill cotton cloth, similar to denim, its name deriving from the stockinette weave.

stocking (T) A fine, machine-knitted fabric, often used for 'elastic' (stretchable) men's breeches.

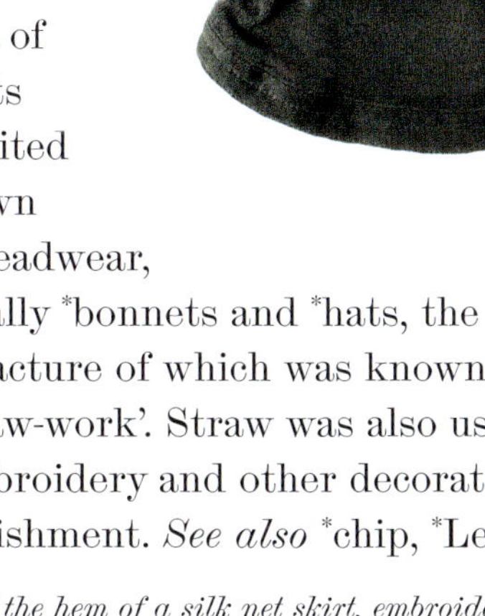

Cuff of dress breeches made from black silk stocking, c.1800–15

straw The dried stems or stalks of cereals, chiefly wheat, barley, oats and rye. In dress, straw was *plaited together to make tapes, then sewn into *headwear, especially *bonnets and *hats, the manufacture of which was known as 'straw-work'. Straw was also used for embroidery and other decorative embellishment. *See also* *chip, *Leghorn.

Detail of the hem of a silk net skirt, embroidered with straw, c.1820

strings Tapes or ties used to tie together the cuffs of breeches, the necklines of gowns, and the like.

stuff A general term for a plain- or twill-woven wool or *worsted fabric, especially thin, light types of cloth, popular for women's day dress and lighter than that used for men's tailored garments. Contemporary accounts also confusingly include silk stuffs, which can mean a textile woven from two fibres, as was common. Stuff was popular for day dress, *'undress' or 'dishabille'. 'Worsted' as a term for the fabric, as well as the fibre from which it was made, was slowly superseding 'stuff' by the Regency period. *See also* *Norwich stuff, *calimanco.

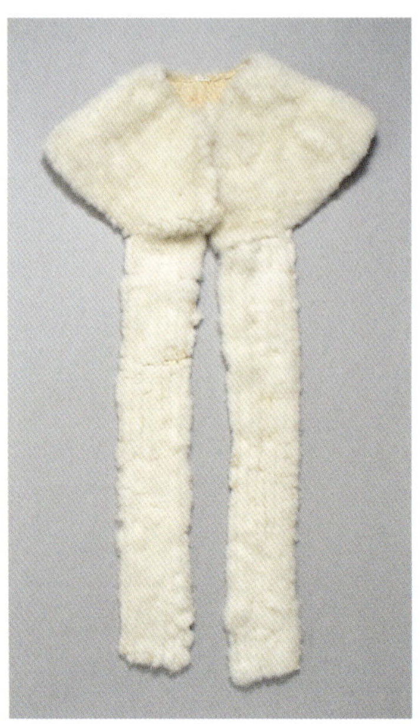

superfine The highest grade of woollen cloth, heavily fulled, the surface raised and cropped to produce a fabric with a soft feel and lustrous appearance; it was used in tailored garments, especially men's *coats.

swansdown (1) The soft under-plumage of the swan, used as a trimming. (2) A cloth made of wool woven with silk or cotton; dyed in many different colours or printed, it was popular for *waistcoats. (3) *See* *swanskin.

Swansdown tippet lined with figured silk, 1800–25

swanskin A thick, fleecy, napped, *twill cotton cloth, similar to *flannel, and confusingly also referred to as 'swansdown'; it was used for undergarments, *gaiters, *jackets and other functional clothing.

tabbinet [tabanet, tabinet] A kind of *poplin with a silk warp and a woollen weft, often with a watered or 'tabbied' finish. The best quality came from Ireland.

French striped tabbinet, 'for morning or domestic wear', January 1815

taffeta [taffety] A crisp, plain-weave fabric, woven with highly twisted threads of 'hard' (gummed) silk, having a tight finish and a somewhat glossy surface.

tambour [tambour work] A form of chain-stitch embroidery, worked in silk or cotton threads with a tambour hook, usually on translucent fabrics such as *muslin, *net and *gauze.

Indian muslin dress with white cotton tambour work (detail), c.1805–10

thread Generally (when not otherwise qualified), a sewing thread or knitting yarn made from linen, as in 'thread stockings' or 'a skein of thread'.

thread button Any button made from a metal ring wrapped across with linen thread; *see* *Dorset button. *See also* *Singleton button.

Linen thread button, 1800–15

tiffany [tiffiny] A very fine, thin, transparent silk or *gauze, sometimes slightly glazed or stiffened with gum.

tinsel (1) An alloy of copper and zinc with a lesser proportion than brass, forming a metal that imitates gold in its appearance and malleability ('yellow tinsel'), or an alloy of silver and copper, to imitate silver ('white tinsel'), made into a thin flat plate strip and used for embroidery, in weaving

Sample of satin tissue with silver, gold and white and yellow tinsel threads, made by Jourdain and John Ham, Spitalfields, 1816

and to cover buttons; or twisted around a fibre core to make a metallic thread. Silver could be 'tinselled' to give a gold surface. (2) A silk, wool or *tissue woven with tinsel thread to create metallic, reflective patterns. (3) Lace made with tinsel thread. All tinsel textiles were cheaper than those incorporating higher-quality glittering materials, and were used extensively in the theatre and for fancy dress, to imitate luxury fabrics.

tissue A silk fabric with a satin ground and an additional weft to create ornamental patterns, usually with silver, gold, gilt or *tinsel threads woven through – hence 'silver tissue' and 'gold tissue'; it was used in *evening dress and *court dress. *See* image for *tinsel.

toilenette [toilenet, toilinet] A cloth with a cotton or silk warp and a woollen weft, popular for waistcoats.

tulle [tule] The French word for machine-woven, hexagonal silk net, more popular in England after 1815. The name derives from the French town where the net was manufactured. *See* *bobbin net and *patent net.

twill A weave in which the warp thread passes over two or more weft threads before passing under (and vice versa), producing regular diagonal ridges on the fabric's surface (*cf.* *plain weave).

twist Plied, stout silk thread, used for making buttonholes and other functional but decorative parts of dress; or for covering wooden bases to make twist *buttons.

Valenciennes lace A handmade *bobbin-lace made first at Valenciennes in France and then in Belgium, characterised by having the lozenge-shaped mesh ground and pattern made at the same time, and the pattern resembling fabric with no cording around the design. Although expensive, and worn frequently in women's *court dress, it was less valued than *Brussels or *Mechlin lace, and considered a thick, strong lace by comparison.

Border of handmade Valenciennes lace with a diamond ground, 19th century

Vandyke Any trimming or accessory finished with V-shaped edging, which could be fabric cut into this shape, or something applied; the shape was inspired by the collars depicted in portraits by the seventeenth-century artist Anthony van Dyck (1599–1641).

'Green satin striped sarsnet frock . . . trimmed with Vandyke lace'. 'Half Dress', November 1814

velveret A striped or ribbed fabric of cotton warp and silk weft, often ribbed; it was popular for men's dress.

velvet A costly all-silk fabric with a short, fine pile, called the nap, shag or velveting. It came in variations of plain, *figured, branched (long branch-like shapes made in pile on a satin ground), shorn, striped, and cut (a ground of *taffeta or *gros de Tours figured with velvet). Imitations of velvet included the coarser, usually woollen *plush, cotton *velveret, and *shag. The fabric's density made it a popular choice for winter fashions.

Epaulette sleeve on a blue velvet spencer, c.*1818*

vicuna [vigogna, vigonia, vigonia cassimere, vicugna, vicunna] Fabric made from the very fine, delicate wool of the vicuña (*Lama vicugna*), finer than *lama wool. These textiles were sometimes adulterated with sheep's wool. The costly fibre was imported from South America and woven in Spain; an imitation textile in *cashmere or sheep wool was called castorine.

wadding [French wadding] A light, fluffy woollen or vegetable-fibre filling material, used for padding outer garments and *gown hems.

wash-leather A soft kind of leather, usually of split sheepskin, dressed to imitate *chamois leather; used for glove linings and stocking foot linings, for *under waistcoats (M), and in cleaning clothes.

whalebone [baleen, baleine] Fine keratin extrusions from the jaw of baleen whales; the material was used as flexible boning, especially in *stays and *corsets.

willow Shavings of willow withies plaited together in strips and used to make *headwear; a kind of *chip.

wool The fine, soft, curly hair forming the fleecy coat of the domesticated sheep (and similar animals). The short soft under-hair or down forming part of the coat of certain hairy or furry animals. For textiles made from wool, *see* *alepine, *alpaca, *angora, *baize, *barragan, *bearskin, *beaver, *broadcloth, *calimanco, *camlet, *carmelite, *cashmere, *chambray, *cloth, *crape, *drugget, *duffel, *flannel, *frieze, *galloon, *grogram, *hunter, *kersey, *kerseymere, *lama, *linsey-wolsey, *list, *Melton, *merino, *mohair, *moreen, *Norwich crape, *plush, *rateen, *satinet, *say, *serge, *stuff, *superfine, *swansdown (2), *tabbinet, *vicuna, *wadding.

worsted The combed, long-staple fibres of a fleece, which are smoother, shinier and more durable than the short-staple, fluffy wool; any thread or fabric made from these fibres. Fabrics made from worsted fibres are sometimes described as 'hard'. For textiles made from worsted, *see* *baize, *barragan, *bombazet, *bombazine, *calimanco, *carmelite, *crewel, *drugget, *everlasting, *florentine, *hard tartan, *lustre, *Norwich crape, *Norwich stuff, *plush, *poplin, *prunella, *satinet, *serge, *shag, *shalloon, *stuff.

zephyrene [zephyreene, zephyrine] A thin, light, soft silk *dress fabric, invented in the late 1810s.

NOTES

1 Elizabeth Gaskell, 'A Fear for the Future', *Fraser's Magazine* (1859): n.p.

2 *The Lady's Monthly Museum; or, Polite Repository of Amusement and Instruction*, vol. 1 (1798): 2.

3 By the Rev. B—C—. 1810 pocketbook, p. 7. Kent Family History Centre, U.951/F.24/1–69.

4 *La Belle Assemblée; or, Bell's Court and Fashionable Magazine*, vol. II (1806): 442.

5 A Lady of Distinction [Mary Hill], *The Mirror of the Graces; or, the English Lady's Costume*, 2nd edn (London: B. Crosby and Co., 1811), p. 25.

6 *The Mirror of the Graces*, p. 95.

7 *The Repository of Arts, Literature, Commerce, Manufactures, Fashions, and Politics*, vol. I (1812): 180.

8 Anonymous, *Dress and Address*, 2nd edn (London: J.J. Stockdale, 1819), p. 50.

9 *The Repository of Arts*, vol. I (1816): 177.

10 Anonymous, *A Book Explaining the Ranks and Dignities of British Society. Intended Chiefly for the Instruction of Young Persons* (London: Tabart & Co.; Heney & Haddon, 1809), pp. 110–12.

11 Anonymous, 'General Observations on Fashion and Dress', *La Belle Assemblée*, vol. IV (1811): 213.

12 *Norfolk Chronicle* (March 1795): n.p.

13 Mr [Richard] Fenton and Samuel Rogers, *Memoirs of an Old Wig* (London: Longman, Hurst, Rees, Orme, and Brown, 1815), p. 2.

14 Penelope Byrde, *The Male Image: Men's Fashion in Britain 1300–1970* (London: B.T. Batsford, 1979), p. 94.

15 Anne Hollander, *Seeing Through Clothes* (Berkeley: University of California Press, 1993), p. 348.

16 Miles Lambert, 'The Dandy in Thackeray's "Vanity Fair" and "Pendennis": An Early Victorian View of the Regency Dandy', *Costume*, vol. 22, no. 1 (1988): 60.

17 'Morning Walking Dresses for Ladies & Gentlemen for March 1807', *Le Beau Monde* (March 1807): n.p.

18 See J.M.L., 'To My Night Cap', in *La Belle Assemblée*, vol. II (1806): 381.

19 *Norfolk Chronicle* (March 1795): n.p.

20 *The Mirror of the Graces*, pp. 89–90.

21 *The New Bon Ton Magazine; or, Telescope of the Times*, vol. II (1820): 132.

22 [John Souter,] *The Book of Trades, or, Library of the Useful Arts*, Part II (London: Tabart and Co., 1806), p. 28.

23 *The Book of Trades*, pp. 26–7.

24 Anonymous, *The Whole Art of Dress! Or, The Road to Elegance and Fashion, at the Enormous Saving of Thirty Per Cent!!! Being a Treatise Upon That Essential and Much-Cultivated Requisite of the Present Day, Gentlemen's Costume . . . by a Cavalry Officer* (London: Effingham Wilson, 1830), p. 97.

25 Anonymous, 'Wigs', *The New Monthly Magazine and Universal Register*, vol. V (1822): 46.

26 [John Souter,] *The Book of Trades, or, Library of the Useful Arts*, Part II (London: Tabart and Co., 1806), pp. 189–90.

27 John Armstrong (ed.), *The Young Woman's Guide to Virtue, Economy, and Happiness; Being an Improved and Pleasant Directory for Cultivating the Heart and Understanding; with a Complete and Elegant System of Domestic Cookery* (Newcastle upon Tyne: Mackenzie & Dent, 1817), p. 342.

28 James Jennings, *The Family Cyclopædia; Being a Manual of Useful and Necessary Knowledge, Alphabetically Arranged; Comprising All the Recent Inventions, Discoveries, and Improvements in Domestic Economy, Agriculture, and Chemistry, Etc* (London: Sherwood, Gilbert, and Piper, 1822), p. 317.

29 *The Mirror of the Graces*, p. 61.

30 See John Scott and John Taylor (eds), 'On Fashions', *The London Magazine*, vol. 12 (1825): 585–92.

31 Jane Austen, *Northanger Abbey*, vol. I, chapter 2.

32 See Hilary Davidson, 'The Unknown Lady's Account Book; or, Mrs. Topham's Treasure, Being a Tale of Historical Deduction, True in All Particulars', *The Female Spectator* [Chawton House], vol. 1, no. 2 (2015): 6–9.

33 See Deb Salisbury (ed.), *Fabric à la Romantic Regency: A Glossary of Fabrics from Original Sources 1795–1836* (Abbott, TX: The Mantua-Maker Historical Sewing Patterns, 2013), p. 139.

34 Thomas Hancock, *Personal Narrative of the Origin and Progress of the Caoutchouc or India-Rubber Manufacture in England* (London: Longman, Brown, Green, Longmans, & Roberts, 1857), p. 4.

35 Text from 1804, quoted in Salisbury (ed.), *Fabric à la Romantic Regency*, p. 128.

36 *Manchester Iris*, 5 July 1823, quoted in Salisbury (ed.), *Fabric à la Romantic Regency*, p. 130.

37 Anthony F. M. Willich, *The Domestic Encyclopædia; or, A Dictionary of Facts, and Useful Knowledge*, vol. III (London: Murray and Highley; Vernor and Hood; G. Kearsley; H.D. Symonds and Thomas Hurst; and the author, 1802), p. 253.

38 *The Penny Cyclopædia of the Society for the Diffusion of Useful Knowledge*, vol. XIX (London: Charles Knight and Co., 1841), p. 492.

BIBLIOGRAPHY

A Lady, *The Workwoman's Guide, Containing Instructions in Cutting Out and Completing Articles of Wearing Apparel, by a Lady* (London: Simpkin Marshall and Co., 1840)

A Lady of Distinction [Mary Hill], *The Mirror of the Graces; or, the English Lady's Costume*, 2nd edn (London: B. Crosby and Co., 1811)

Anonymous, *A Book Explaining the Ranks and Dignities of British Society. Intended Chiefly for the Instruction of Young Persons* (London: Tabart & Co.; Heney & Haddon, 1809)

Anonymous, *A Visit to the Bazaar* (London: Bodley Head, 1818)

Anonymous, *Dress and Address*, 2nd edn (London: J.J. Stockdale, 1819)

Anonymous, *The Whole Art of Dress! Or, The Road to Elegance and Fashion, at the Enormous Saving of Thirty Per Cent!!! Being a Treatise Upon That Essential and Much-Cultivated Requisite of the Present Day, Gentlemen's Costume . . . by a Cavalry Officer* (London: Effingham Wilson, 1830)

Armstrong, John (ed.), *The Young Woman's Guide to Virtue, Economy, and Happiness; Being an Improved and Pleasant Directory for Cultivating the Heart and Understanding; with a Complete and Elegant System of Domestic Cookery* (Newcastle upon Tyne: Mackenzie & Dent, 1817)

Badcock, John, *Slang: A Dictionary of the Turf, the Ring, the Chase, the Pit, or Bon-Ton, and the Varieties of Life, Forming the Completest and Most Authentic Lexicon Balatronicum Hitherto Offered to the Notice of the Sporting World* (London: T. Hughes, 1823)

Bassett, Lynne Z., *Gothic to Goth: Romantic Era Fashion & Its Legacy* (Hartford, CT: Wadsworth Atheneum Museum of Art, 2016)

Bennett, David, and Daniela Mascetti, *Understanding Jewellery* (Woodbridge: Antique Collectors' Club, 1994)

Booth, David, *An Analytical Dictionary of the English Language* (London: J. & C. Adlard, 1830)

Byrde, Penelope, *The Male Image: Men's Fashion in Britain 1300–1970* (London: B.T. Batsford, 1979)

Byrde, Penelope, '"That Frightful Unbecoming Dress": Clothes for Spa Bathing at Bath', *Costume*, vol. 21, no. 1 (1987): 44–56

Caron, Auguste, *The Lady's Toilette: Containing a Critical Examination of the Nature of Beauty, and of the Causes by Which It Is Impaired: with Instructions for Preserving It to Advanced Age; an Historical Sketch of the Fashions of France and England; Directions for Dressing with Taste and Elegance; and Receipts for Preparing All the Best and Most Harmless Cosmetics Proper for a Lady's Use* (London: W.H. Wyatt, 1808)

Carter, Alison J., *Regency to Art Nouveau: Taste and Fashion in European Jewellery from the Eighteenth to the Twentieth Centuries. The Hull Grundy Gift to Cheltenham Art Gallery and Museums*, vol. I (Cheltenham: Cheltenham Art Gallery and Museums, 1986)

Caulfeild, Sophia Frances Anne, *The Dictionary of Needlework: An Encyclopædia of Artistic, Plain, and Fancy Needlework, Dealing Fully with the Details of All the Stitches Employed, the Method of Working, the Materials Used, the Meaning of Technical Terms, and, Where Necessary, Tracing the Origin and History of the Various Works Described* (London: L. Upcott Gill, 1885)

Clabburn, Pamela, 'A Provincial Milliner's Shop in 1785', *Costume*, vol. 11, no. 1 (1977): 100–12

Clabburn, Pamela, *Shawls* (Princes Risborough: Shire Publications, 2002)

Cumming, Valerie, C.W. Cunnington, and P.E. Cunnington, *The Dictionary of Fashion History*, updated, supplement edn (London: Bloomsbury Visual Arts, 2022)

Cunnington, C. Willett, *Feminine Attitudes in the Nineteenth Century* (New York: Haskell House Publishers, 1973)

Curtis, Thomas, *The London Encyclopædia: Or, Universal Dictionary of Science, Art, Literature, and Practical Mechanics, Comprising a Popular View of the Present State of Knowledge* (London: Thomas Tegg, 1829)

Davidson, Hilary, 'Dress & Dressmaking: Material Evolution in Regency Dress Construction', in *Material Literacy in Eighteenth-Century Britain: A Nation of Makers*, ed. Serena Dyer and Chloe Wigston Smith (London: Bloomsbury Academic, 2020), pp. 173–94

Davidson, Hilary, 'Looking Back Through Fashion: Regency Romances and a "Jumble of Styles"', in *The Edinburgh Companion to Romanticism and the Arts*, ed. Maureen McCue and Sophie Thomas (Edinburgh: Edinburgh University Press, 2022), pp. 502–22

Dawes, Ginny Redington, with Olivia Collings, *Georgian Jewellery 1714–1830* (Woodbridge: Antique Collectors' Club, 2007)

Eaton, Linda, *Printed Textiles: British and American Cottons and Linens 1700–1850* (New York: The Monacelli Press, 2014)

Faber Oestreich, Kate, 'Critical Decades: Textiles and Material Culture in *Jane Eyre* and Three Recent Adaptations', *Brontë Studies*, vol. 49, no. 4 (2024): 313–29

Farrell, Jeremy, *Socks & Stockings* (London: B.T. Batsford, 1992)

Farrell, Jeremy, *Umbrellas & Parasols* (London: B.T. Batsford, 1985)

Felkin, William, *A History of the Machine-Wrought Hosiery and Lace Manufactures* (London: Longmans, Green, and Co., 1867)

Fenton, Mr [Richard], and Samuel Rogers, *Memoirs of an Old Wig* (London: Longman, Hurst, Rees, Orme, and Brown, 1815)

Gere, Charlotte, Judy Rodoe, Hugh Tait and Timothy Wilson, *The Art of the Jeweller: A Catalogue of the Hull Grundy Gift to the British Museum: Jewellery, Engraved Gems, and Goldsmiths' Work*, ed. Hugh Tait (London: British Museum Publications, 1984)

Greenberg, Hope, 'Exploring the Austen-Era Toque', June 2022: www.uvm.edu/~hag/2022-jasp-toque-history-catalog.pdf (accessed 17 February 2025)

Grimble, Frances (ed.), *The Lady's Stratagem: A Repository of 1820s Directions for the Toilet, Mantua-Making, Stay-Making, Millinery & Etiquette* (San Francisco: Lavolta Press, 2009)

Grose, Francis, *A Classical Dictionary of the Vulgar Tongue* [1788] (London: S. Hooper, 1811)

Hancock, Thomas, *Personal Narrative of the Origin and Progress of the Caoutchouc or India-Rubber Manufacture in England* (London: Longman, Brown, Green, Longmans, & Roberts, 1857)

Harmuth, Louis, *Dictionary of Textiles* (Cambridge: Cambridge Scholars Publishing, 1915)

Harte, Negley B., 'On Rees's *Cyclopaedia* as a Source for the History of the Textile Industries in the Early Nineteenth Century', *Textile History*, vol. 5, no. 1 (1974): 119–27

Hollander, Anne, *Seeing Through Clothes* (Berkeley: University of California Press, 1993)

The India Office List (H.M. Stationery Office, 1828)

J.M.L., 'To My Night Cap', in *La Belle Assemblée; or, Bell's Court and Fashionable Magazine*, vol. II (1806)

Johnson, Samuel, *Johnson's Dictionary of the English Language in Miniature*, ed. Rev. Joseph Hamilton, 9th edn (London: Longman, 1798)

Kelly, Ian, *Beau Brummell: The Ultimate Dandy* (London: Hodder and Stoughton, 2005)

Kingsbury, Benjamin, *A Treatise on Razors; in Which the Weight, Shape, and Temper of a Razor, the Means of Keeping it in Order, and the Manner of Using it, are Particularly Considered* (London: E. Blackader, 1797)

La Belle Assemblée; or, Bell's Court and Fashionable Magazine (1806–37)

The Lady's Monthly Museum; or, Polite Repository of Amusement and Instruction (1798–1832)

Lambert, Miles, 'The Dandy in Thackeray's "Vanity Fair" and "Pendennis": An Early Victorian View of the Regency Dandy', *Costume*, vol. 22, no. 1 (1988): 60–69

Lemire, Beverly, *The British Cotton Trade, 1660–1815* (London: Pickering & Chatto, 2010)

Lemire, Beverly, *Cotton* (London: Bloomsbury, 2013)

Lévi-Strauss, Monique, *The Cashmere Shawl* (New York: Abrams, 1988)

MacFarquhar, Colin, and George Gleig, *Encyclopædia Britannica; or, A Dictionary of Arts, Sciences, and Miscellaneous Literature* (Edinburgh: A. Bell and C. MacFarquhar, 1797)

Maeder, Edward, *An Elegant Art: Fashion & Fantasy in the Eighteenth Century. Los Angeles County Museum of Art Collection of Costumes and Textiles* (Los Angeles: Los Angeles County Museum of Art, 1983)

Maskiell, Michelle, 'Consuming Kashmir: Shawls and Empires, 1500–2000', in *Fashion: Critical and Primary Sources*, vol. 3 (The Nineteenth Century), ed. Peter McNeil (Oxford and New York: Berg, 2009), pp. 207–40

Matthews David, Alison, 'War and Wellingtons: Military Footwear in the Age of Empire', in *Shoes: A History from Sandals to Sneakers*, ed. Giorgio Riello and Peter McNeil (Oxford: Berg, 2006), pp. 116–37

McCormack, Matthew, *Shoes and the Georgian Man* (London: Bloomsbury Visual Arts, 2025)

Montefiore, Joshua, *A Commercial Dictionary: Containing the Present State of Mercantile Law, Practice, and Custom Intended for the Use of the Cabinet, the Counting-House, and the Library* (London: Printed for the author, 1803)

Mortimer, Thomas, *A General Dictionary of Commerce, Trade, and Manufactures: Exhibiting their Present State in Every Part of the World; and Carefully Comp. from the Latest and Best Authorities* (London: R. Phillips, 1810)

Neckclothitania; or, Tietania: Being an Essay on Starchers, by One of the Cloth (London: J.J. Stockdale, 1818)

The New Bon Ton Magazine; or, Telescope of the Times, vol. II (1820)

Nicholson, William, *The British Encyclopedia, or Dictionary of Arts and Sciences* (London: Longman, Hurst, Rees, and Orme, 1809)

Oxford English Dictionary: www.oed.com/ (accessed 17 February 2025)

The Penny Cyclopædia of the Society for the Diffusion of Useful Knowledge, vols. I–XXVII, esp. vol. XIX (London: Charles Knight and Co., 1841)

Rees, Abraham, *The Cyclopaedia; or, Universal Dictionary of Arts, Sciences, and Literature*, vol. XL (London: Longman, Hurst, Rees, Orme, and Brown, 1810)

Rees, John F., *The Art and Mystery of a Cordwainer; or, An Essay on the Principles and Practice of Boot and Shoe-Making* (London: Gale, Curtis, and Fenner, 1813)

Rehman, Sherry, and Naheed Jafri, *The Kashmiri Shawl: From Jamavar to Paisley* (Woodbridge: Antique Collectors' Club, 2006)

The Repository of Arts, Literature, Commerce, Manufactures, Fashions, and Politics (1809–29)

Ribeiro, Aileen, *Facing Beauty: Painted Women & Cosmetic Art* (London and New Haven, CT: Yale University Press, 2011)

Riello, Giorgio, *Cotton: The Fabric That Made the Modern World* (West Nyack, NY: Cambridge University Press, 2013)

Riello, Giorgio, *A Foot in the Past: Consumers, Producers and Footwear in the Long Eighteenth Century* (Oxford and New York: Pasold Research Fund/Oxford University Press, 2006)

Riello, Giorgio, and Prasannan Parthasarathi, *The Spinning World: A Global History of Cotton Textiles, 1200–1850* (Oxford and New York: Pasold Research Fund/Oxford University Press, 2009)

Scarisbrick, Diana, *Jewellery in Britain, 1066–1837: A Documentary, Social, Literary and Artistic Survey* (Norwich: Michael Russell, 1994)

Schechter, Ronald, 'Gothic Thermidor: The *Bals des victimes*, the Fantastic, and the Production of Historical Knowledge in Post-Terror France', *Representations*, vol. 61 (1998): 78–94

Sholtz, Mackenzie, and Kristen Miller Zohn, '"A Staymaker of Edinburgh": Corsetry in the Age of Austen', *Persuasions: The Jane Austen Journal On-Line*, vol. 41, no. 1 (2020): https://jasna.org/publications-2/persuasions-online/vol-41-no-1/sholtz-zohn/ (accessed 17 February 2025)

Sinclair, Sir John, *The Code of Health and Longevity; or, A Concise View of the Principles Calculated for the Preservation of Health, and the*

Attainment of Long Life, 3rd edn (London: Printed for the author, 1816)

[Souter, John,] *The Book of Trades, or, Library of the Useful Arts*, Part II (London: Tabart and Co., 1806)

Styles, John, *The Dress of the People: Everyday Fashion in Eighteenth-Century England* (London and New Haven, CT: Yale University Press, 2007)

Styles, John, 'Re-Fashioning Industrial Revolution: Fibres, Fashion and Technical Innovation in British Cotton Textiles, 1600–1780', in *La moda come motore economico: innovazione di processo e prodotto, nuove strategie commerciali, comportamento dei consumatori / Fashion as an Economic Engine: Process and Product Innovation, Commercial Strategies, Consumer Behavior*, ed. Giampiero Nigro (Florence: Firenze University Press, 2022), pp. 45–71

Swann, June, *Shoes* (London: B.T. Batsford, 1982)

Tozer, Jane, 'Cunnington's Interpretation of Dress', *Costume*, vol. 20, no. 1 (1986): 1–17

Upright, Solomon [pseud.], *Hints to the Bearers of Walking-Sticks and Umbrellas* (London: John Murray, 1809)

Walker, John, *A Critical Pronouncing Dictionary and Expositor of the English Language . . .* (London: T. Cadell and W. Davies, 1810)

Webster, Thomas, *An Encyclopædia of Domestic Economy: Comprising Such Subjects as are Most Immediately Connected with House-keeping . . .* (New York: Harper & Brothers, 1845)

Wilcox, David, 'The Clothing of a Georgian Banker, Thomas Coutts: A Story of Museum Dispersal', *Costume*, vol. 26, no. 1 (2012): 17–54

Wilcox, David, 'The Clothing of a Regency Poet, Lord Byron (1788–1824)', *Costume*, vol. 55, no. 2 (2021): 212–39

Wilcox, David, 'The Clothing of a Regency Poet, Lord Byron (1788–1824): A Period of Exile 1816–1824', *Costume*, vol. 56, no. 2 (2022): 151–82

Willich, Anthony Florian Madinger, and James Mease, *The Domestic Encyclopædia; or, A Dictionary of Facts, and Useful Knowledge, Comprehending a Concise View of the Latest Discoveries, Inventions, and Improvements, Chiefly Applicable to Rural and Domestic Economy*, expanded edn (Philadelphia: W.Y. Birch and A. Small, 1804)

Withey, Alun, *Concerning Beards: Facial Hair, Health and Practice in England 1650–1900*, Facialities: Interdisciplinary Approaches to the Human Face (London: Bloomsbury Academic, 2021)

Withey, Alun, '"Hairy Honours of their Chins": Whiskers and Masculinity in Early Nineteenth-Century Britain', *Social History*, vol. 47, no. 4 (2022): 395–418

ILLUSTRATION CREDITS

WOMEN'S HAIRSTYLES *(pp. 138–40)*

undressed hair	Ann Mee, *Jane, Countess of Galloway*, *c.*1812–14
1795	George Engleheart, *A Lady of the Blunt Family*, *c.*1795
1796	*Gallery of Fashion*, vol. III, March 1796
1797	Sir William Beechey, *Princess Sophia*, 1796–97
1798	Ann Frankland Lewis, *Collection of English Original Watercolour Drawings*: Plate 24, 1798
1799	Ann Frankland Lewis, *Collection of English Original Watercolour Drawings*: Plate 25, 1799
1800	William Wood, *Elizabeth Bourke*, 1800
1801	John Russell, *Mrs William Pierrepont (née Maria Salter)*, 1801
1802	*Gallery of Fashion*, vol. VIII, February 1802
1803	John Downman, *Miss Campbell*, 1803
1804	John Dowman, *Portrait of a Lady, identified as Eliza Were Holdsworth*, 1804
1805	George Engleheart, *Portrait miniature of an unknown woman*, 1805
1806	John Constable, *Head of a Young Woman*, 1806
1807	Morning & Evening Dresses in Nov. 1, 1807, *La Belle Assemblée*, December 1807
1808	*Le Beau Monde*, February 1808
1809	John Smart, *Miss Mary Tadman*, 1809
1810	Evening or Full Dress, *The Repository of Arts*, June 1810

1811 A section from Barbara Johnson's album, folio X
1812 Andrew Geddes, *The Artist's Sister (Anne Geddes)*, 1812
1813 Adam Buck, *The Artist and his Family*, 1813
1814 John Cox Dillman Engleheart, *Eliza Bridgeman O'Brien (née Willyams)*, 1814
1815 Archibald Skirving, *Lady Pringle, née Emilia Anne Macleod*, 1815
1816 Rolinda Sharples, *The Artist and her Mother*, 1816
1817 After George Dawe, *Princess Charlotte of Wales*, 1817
1818 Rolinda Sharples, *The Cloak-Room, Clifton Assembly Rooms*, 1818
1819 Sir Thomas Lawrence, *Lady Selina Meade*, 1819
1820 Edward Nash, Sara Coleridge; *Edith May Warter*, 1820

MEN'S HAIRSTYLES

(p. 141)

1798 Henry Bone, *Robert Cathcart, Esq.*, 1798
1800 John Singleton Copley, *Colonel William Fitch and His Sisters Sarah and Ann Fitch*, 1800/10
1802 Thomas Heaphy, *Portrait of Hastings Nathaniel Middleton with his country seat beyond*, 1802
1805 George Dance, *Portrait of a Young Man*, 1805
1808 Samuel John Stump, *Henry Siddons*, 1808
1812 George Chinnery, *John Lyon*, 1812
1816 Sir George Hayter, *Prince Leopold of Saxe-Coburg-Saalfeld*, 1816
1819 John Linnell, *Portrait of a Man*, 1819

PICTURE CREDITS

Courtesy 1st Dibs **162**, **169** (bottom)

Courtesy Bally Shoe Museum, Schoenenwerd, Switzerland **210** (top)

Courtesy Birmingham Museum of Art. Museum purchase with funds donated by James A. Simpson, William M. Spencer, Jr., and The Women's Day Lecture Series, 1966.143 **160**

Courtesy of Bonhams **141** (1802)

Bridgeman Images: © Bristol Museums, Galleries & Archives/Bridgeman Images **65**, **140** (1816, 1818); Photo © CSG CIC Glasgow Museums Collection/Bridgeman Images **79** (bottom); © Fashion Museum Bath/Bridgeman Images **58** (top); © Maidstone Museum and Bentlif Art Gallery/© Maidstone Museum and Art Gallery/Bridgeman Images **145** (top); © Philip Mould Ltd, London/ Bridgeman Images **153**, **159** (middle); © The Fitzwilliam Museum, Cambridge **139** (1809); Bridgeman

Images **139** (1804); National Galleries of Scotland. Bequeathed by Kenneth Sanderson 1944. Photo by Antonia Reeve **115**; National Maritime Museum, Greenwich, London. Bridgeman Images **138** (1801); Photo © Photo Josse/Bridgeman Images **45** (top)

British Museum: © The Trustees of the British Museum **46**, **76** (top), **120**

Courtesy of Candice Hern **47**, **74** (top), **139** (1808)

Courtesy of Chorley's Auctioneers Limited UK/Photo by Scott Capener **53**

Courtesy of Christie's **140** (1819)

Colchester and Ipswich Museums Service: Ipswich Borough Council Collection **85**

Cooper Hewitt, Smithsonian Design Museum: Cooper Hewitt, Smithsonian Design Museum Collection **73** (top); Gift of Frederick Saal in honour of Dr. and Mrs. Joseph Saal, **168**; Gift of I. Townsend Burden, Jr., **203**; Gift of Mrs. George Nichols from the collection of her mother, Mrs. J.P. Morgan, **211** (bottom), **227** (top); Gift of Mrs. John Innes Kane, **57** (bottom)

Hargesheimer Kunstauktionen Düsseldorf; photograph: Udo Fischer **42** (top)

Hilary Davidson: **43** (top), **48** (bottom), **51** (bottom), **59** (bottom), **62** (top), **63**, **97**, **104**, **108** (top), **119** (bottom), **122** (bottom), **128** (top), **146**, **183**, **189** (top), **190**, **192** (bottom), **200** (both), **202**, **205**, **207** (top), **216** (bottom), **217** (bottom), **219** (both), **221**, **222** (bottom), **223** (both), **224** (middle and bottom), **225** (both)

Hilary Davidson/New York Public Library: **39**, **45** (bottom), **49** (bottom), **69** (top), **109** (top), **174**, **191** (top), **204** (both), **206**, **210** (bottom), **211** (top), **217** (top), **224** (middle)

The J. Paul Getty Museum, Los Angeles **103**, **112** (bottom)

Courtesy of Jane Austen's House. Photograph by Peter Smith **162**

Courtesy of Kerry Taylor Auctions: **69** (bottom), **72** (top), **116** (top), **122** (top), **191** (bottom), **195**, **214**, **220**, **222** (top)

Los Angeles County Museum of Art (LACMA) www.lacma.org: Costume Council Fund, **82** (top), **138** (1796), **201**; Gift of Dr. and Mrs. Gerald Labiner, **38**, **49** (top), **54** (bottom), **55**, **57** (top), **59**, **70**, **80**, **82** (bottom), **86**, **88**, **139** (1807), **145** (bottom), **163** (top), **227** (bottom); Gift of Mrs. Hazel Steadman Brukhardt, **78** (top); Purchased with funds provided by Cecile Bartman **98** (bottom); Purchased with funds provided by Suzanne A. Saperstein and Michael and Ellen Michelson, with additional funding from the Costume Council, the Edgerton Foundation, Gail and Gerald Oppenheimer, Maureen H. Shapiro, Grace Tsao, and Lenore and Richard Wayne, **52**, **71** (bottom left), **184** (top), **213**, **216** (top)

London Museum, © The Board of Governors of the London Museum, **81** (top)

The Metropolitan Museum of Art, New York: Brooklyn Museum Costume Collection at The Metropolitan Museum of Art, Gift of the Brooklyn Museum, 2009; Augustus Graham School of Design Fund, 1976 **58** (bottom), **71** (bottom left), **83** (middle), **129**; Costume Institute

Benefit Fund, 1999, **77** (top); Gift of George A. Hearn, 1906, **26**; Gift of Mrs. Charles Wrightsman, in honour of Philippe de Montebello, 2004, **164**; Gift of Mrs. DeWitt Clinton Cohen, 1941, **79** (top); Gift of Mrs. Guy Fairfax Cary, in memory of her mother, Mrs. Burke Roche, 1949, **121** (bottom); Gift of Mrs. Jesse H. Metcalf, 1946, **68**; Gift of Olive Shurlock Sjölander, 1975, **64**; Gift of the family of Thomas Coutts, 1908, **106** (bottom), **125** (bottom); Purchase, Gifts in memory of Paul Ettesvold, 1988, **127**; Purchase, Irene Lewisohn Bequest, 1972, **87** (top); Purchase, Isabel Shults Fund, 2020, **215**; The Elisha Whittelsey Collection, The Elisha Whittelsey Fund, 1950, **60**, **67** (top), **74** (bottom), **138** (1796, 1802); The Elisha Whittelsey Collection, The Elisha Whittelsey Fund, 1959, **41**, **128** (bottom)

Musée du Louvre. Photo © RMN-Grand Palais (Musée du Louvre) / Thierry Le Mage **139** (1806)

Museum of Arts and Sciences, Sydney. The Joseph Box Collection **42** (bottom)

National Gallery, London **141** (1800)

National Gallery of Art, Washington DC **124**

National Galleries of Scotland. Presented by Mrs H. F. Rose 1951 **140** (1812)

National Gallery of Victoria, Melbourne. The Schofield Collection. Purchased with the assistance of a special grant from the Government of Victoria, 1974 **66** (top)

© National Maritime Museum, Greenwich, London **198**

© National Portrait Gallery, London: **99**, **140** (1814), **141** (1808), **148**; Bequeathed by Edith May Warter's granddaughter, Mrs E.A.**140** (1820)

National Trust: © National Trust/David Cousins & Sonja Power **144** (bottom); © National Trust/Richard Blakey **112** (top), **208**; © National Trust/Sophia Farley **108** (bottom); © National Trust/Thomas Boggis **40**; © National Trust Images/Matthew Hollow **167** (top)

New York Public Library: Carl H. Pforzheimer Collection of Shelley and His Circle **102**; New York Public Library **50**, **81** (bottom), **98** (top), **105** (top)

Philadelphia Museum of Art: Gift of Mrs. Daniel J. McCarthy, 1955, 1955-1-10, public domain, https://www.philamuseum.org/collection/object/54833 **116** (bottom); Gift of the McNeil Americana Collection, 2008, 1955-1-10, public domain, https://philamuseum.org/collection/object/322598 **144** (top); The George W. Elkins Collection, 1945, E1945-1-1, public domain, https://www.philamuseum.org/collection/object/102998 **123** (top)

Rijksmuseum, Amsterdam: **75** (top), **114**, **125** (bottom); Donation from Mrs. Luchtsinger, **72** (bottom); Rijksmuseum, Amsterdam. E.J. Hodges Bequest, Amsterdam, **44** (top); Gift of A. Baroness van Harinxma thoe Slooten, Amsterdam, **51** (top); Gift of E.S. Kramer, The Hague and J.J. Kramer, The Hague, **75** (bottom); Gift of Jonkvrouw A.C. Teding van Berkhout, Amsterdam and S.F., Baroness van Höevell-Teding van Berkhout, Bergen (Noord-Holland),

54 (top); Gift of Jonkvrouw C.I. Six, 's-Graveland, **76** (bottom), **78** (bottom), **194**, **218**; Gift of W. Fuhri-Snethlage, Haarlem, **77** (bottom); Jonkvrouw A.C.A.J. Clifford Bequest, The Hague, **161** (top), **185**; Mr and Mrs Drucker-Fraser Bequest, Montreux, **87** (bottom); On loan from the Koninklijke Verzamelingen, **181** (top); Purchased with the support of the Flora Fonds/Rijksmuseum Fonds, **61**, **73** (bottom), **83** (top)

Rhode Island School of Design, Courtesy of the RISD Museum, Providence, RI **48** (top), **80** (bottom)

Royal Collection Trust: © Royal Collection Enterprises Limited 2024 | Royal Collection Trust **138** (undressed hair, 1797), **141** (1816), **181** (bottom), **197**

Courtesy of Sian Harlowe Antiques **159** (top)

Courtesy of Sotheby's **170**

Courtesy of Sperlich Jewelry **167** (bottom)

State Library of New South Wales: **126**; State Library of New South Wales, Mitchell Library **138** (1800)

Tate, Presented by Mrs C. FitzHugh 1843. Photo: Tate **156**

University of Illinois at Urbana-Champaign Library, Digital Rare Book Collection, Rare Book & Manuscript Library **101**, **105** (bottom), **130**

© Victoria and Albert Museum, London: **62** (bottom), **119** (top), **139** (1805, 1811), **161** (bottom), **163** (bottom), **165** (both), **166**, **171** (top), **186**, **188** (top), **192** (top), **224** (top); Given by Dame Kathleen Courtney DBE, **56**; Given by Margaret Simeon, **71** (top); Given by Messrs Harrods Ltd, **43** (bottom), **184** (bottom), **228**; Given by Mr Francis Coutts, **109** (bottom), **117**, **118** (top); Given by Spencer G. Perceval, **159** (bottom); Given by the American Friends of the V&A through the generosity of Patricia V. Goldstein, **171** (bottom)

Wikimedia Commons: **84**, **106** (top), **111** (top), **199;** Wikimedia Commons/Dulwich Picture Gallery, London **44** (bottom); Wikimedia Commons/Kimbell Art Museum **123** (bottom); Wikimedia Commons/Royal Collection Trust/© His Majesty Charles III, 2025 **140** (1817)

Winterthur Museum and Library: **182** (both), **187** (both), **189** (bottom), **193**, **207** (bottom), **209**

Yale Center for British Art: Paul Mellon Collection **66** (bottom), **67** (bottom), **83** (bottom), **92**, **111** (bottom), **113**, **121** (top), **138** (1795), **139** (1803), **140** (1813), **141** (1798, 1805, 1812, 1819);

Paul Mellon Fund, in honour of Jane and Richard C. Levin, President of Yale University (1993–2013) **140** (1815)

Yale University Library: Beinecke Rare Book and Manuscript Library **100**; Lewis Walpole Library **118** (bottom), **134**